C000132358

What It Feels Like To Be Me

First published by O Books, 2010
O Books is an imprint of John Hunt Publishing Ltd., The Bothy, Deershot Lodge, Park Lane, Ropley,
Hants, SO24 0BE, UK
office1@o-books.net
www.o-books.net

Distribution in:	South Africa
	Stephan Phillips (pty) Ltd
UK and Europe	Email: orders@stephanphillips.com
Orca Book Services	Tel: 27 21 4489839 Telefax: 27 21 4479879
orders@orcabookservices.co.uk	
Tel: 01202 665432 Fax: 01202 666219	Text copyright Jenny Manson 2009
Int. code (44)	
	Design: Tom Davies
USA and Canada	
NBN	ISBN: 978 1 84694 362 1
custserv@nbnbooks.com	
Tel: 1 800 462 6420 Fax: 1 800 338 4550	All rights reserved. Except for brief quotations
	in critical articles or reviews, no part of this
Australia and New Zealand	book may be reproduced in any manner without
Brumby Books	prior written permission from the publishers.
sales@brumbybooks.com.au	
Tel: 61 3 9761 5535 Fax: 61 3 9761 7095	The rights of Jenny Manson as author have been
	asserted in accordance with the Copyright,
Far East (offices in Singapore, Thailand,	Designs and Patents Act 1988.
Hong Kong, Taiwan)	
Pansing Distribution Pte Ltd	
kemal@pansing.com	A CIP catalogue record for this book is available
Tel: 65 6319 9939 Fax: 65 6462 5761	from the British Library.

Printed by CPI Antony Rowe, Chippenham, Wiltshire

O Books operates a distinctive and ethical publishing philosophy in
all areas of its business, from its global network of authors to
production and worldwide distribution.

What It Feels Like To Be Me

Jenny Manson

To Judy

with best wishes,

Jenny Manson

BOOKS

Winchester, UK
Washington, USA

CONTENTS

Preface

When I was in my early 20s and had just joined the civil service, I realised that what really interested me was what it felt like to be other people. I was curious that people did not talk much about the self within, hiding instead behind their faces and manners. As children, nothing prepares us for being alone in our heads. There is no advice or commiseration offered to help us cope with our internal aloneness and with the puzzle of the consciousness.

I thought at the time of doing a spoken questionnaire on the theme 'What does it feel like to be you?' and started asking questions of a work colleague in his late 50s. He was startled, amused and incredulous at the questions (the one I remember was about his finding himself living with things that he saw as second best), but he told me his truth, was exhilarated and asked for more questions.

I have thought about different approaches ever since. Reading John Updike's memoirs, *Self-Consciousness*, in the 1990s was a revelation. In particular the last essay, 'On Being a Self Forever', struck me as a brilliant description of 'What it feels like to be me'. The sound of John Updike's seemingly true voice in 'On Being a Self Forever' convinced me that a questionnaire would be too constricting a framework for this idea.

It also struck me that when writing letters we tend to say something more revelatory about our selves than in conversation and that letters seem often to be addressed to a generic reader. I heard Will Self on the radio saying that when writing we say who we are while as a reader we form an intimate relationship with the writer.

So I thought I would ask a selection of people to write about themselves with only a minimal structure imposed by me. Again, I was going to put this off until I had more time but I spoke to a few friends who were likely candidates (Simon, Rob and Amelia if I remember), and they all said yes and that they wanted to get going straight away. When finally the project got off the ground, it started racing.

I selected people who are honest and fresh when they talk about themselves. As well as being people I like and trust, they have a sort of innocence – a familiar trait to me, particularly from my father's side of the family – as they think it worthwhile trying to understand the nature of existence.

I sent out a short introductory piece and a series of prompts. Most people found this useful. I explained that I was interested in what it feels like in their heads day to day, in the middle of the night, when with other people, implicitly not in events and achievements.

After some thinking time the majority of the contributors, to my surprise, came up with the goods with very little chasing, mostly in three to six months. The few (mainly women) who did not want to write explained that the place inside their minds was just too painful. Some of these took my suggestion to write at a tangent from what hurts them too much, for example Helen and Rob. One, Simon, approached the theme directly and without equivocation. Others reached an answer by reflecting on various aspects of their lives.

The contributors write about the voices in their heads, their struggle to make sense of things and to live with their memories. This appears to be a neglected area, although it is the universal human condition and it may explain why people are fascinated and excited by it, both as contributors and as potential readers. People of all ages and backgrounds understand what I mean, often just when I tell them the title. Many have asked how it is that no one has thought of this idea before.

There is no disguise as there would be in fiction. Many of the contributors have careers that do not involve a large degree of self-expression, such as jobs in engineering, medicine and the civil service. Yet there is a creative zing in the essays which appeals to the imagination. Some read like autobiographies, some do not at all, but the emphasis is on what it feels like today. In many of the contributions there is recognition of the lasting and poignant nature of childhood memories but the book is not an evocation of childhood.

Compared to therapy there is no exchange with another person and no search for an explanation or cure (although some people describe their search for their self through life). There is no filter: the contributors are speaking to and for themselves. But almost all the contributors have said they found the experience helpful, many describing it as therapeutic. Also, in common with a therapy session, it seems to me that whatever approach the contributors have chosen in answer to my question, it is valid.

In some cases life events have intervened and many contributors said 'stop me now or I will go on changing it forever'. A few have had such dramatic life changes in the last year that they say they would write the piece quite differently now. But I felt, on reading successive versions of their piece – some contributors had more than one go – that the spirit of the person that emerges is a constant, even if it does not feel like that to the writer him/herself.

They have been prepared to bare their souls. For example, Dominic writes that no one shares or understands his memories. Some approach themselves obliquely but many write of their feeling of being an outsider. They put on a good act and often other people would not guess how tenuously they feel they grip on to their place in the world.

Adapting yourself to other people preoccupies several of the writers. This seems to be the hardest thing to hack, especially for the men. Some of these men, even if they are perceived as successful and effective at work, are handicapped by a fear of day-to-day social relations. But a common theme for the women as well is the clash between how they see themselves and how they think they are seen by others.

There is rather little in the book about love and sex. For this perhaps you want the anonymity of fiction. But also it may be that, contrary to the popular view, it is not always or only our intimate relationships that trouble us but, instead, we dwell on the small perceived slights from and misunderstandings about all those other people we knock into every day.

I see the world differently since reading these essays. I have more sympathy for the writers: I liked them all already but now I recognise their insecurities. When I walk in the street these days I imagine I hear the true voices of the people I pass. It is hard not to like someone when you hear their story in their own words. If we heard each other speak in this way we would be more conscious of the insecurities that lurk behind the solid front that most people put on.

I would guess that every sort of reader would identify with someone in the book. The effect on me of reading the pieces was that I had a fellow feeling for them all, seeing their vulnerability and getting a glimpse of those puzzled private worlds. I have already found this helpful in, for example, a clash of views at work.

I wonder if the idea of asking people how it feels to be them could catch on. At times I imagine that it could be a new craze, discussed on talk shows, in lunch breaks at work or on the bus home. In more sober moments I think that taking a direct interest in other people's inner lives has potential for schools, prisons and other institutions.

The Contributors

I have put the pieces in three Parts: *Setting out, Making sense of it all* and *Mulling it over*. In the first part, the youngest contributor is Nina who is 14. The others are Victoria, aged 20, Amelia 29, Stephen 33 and Larry 39.

Between Parts I and II is a poem by Peter Phillips, *Bath Time Butterflies at Boarding School*.

In Part II, the contributors struggling to make sense of it all are Mark, aged 40, Kate 47, Simon 48, Leo and Lia who are both 55 and Dominic 56. Dominic has discovered the close parallel between his piece and contributions to a book about boarding school survivors, *The Making of Them*, by Nick Duffell.

Between Parts II and III is a poem by Dannie Abse, *The Trial*.

In Part III, the contributors who are mulling it over are Uma aged 57, Fran and Richard who are husband and wife and are both 59, Helen and Rob also 59, Colin aged 63 and Julie 85. Since Julie wrote her piece, one of her sons has talked to her and me about what it feels like from his angle: he plans to write his own piece one day.

From the start I have also been interested in how people would interpret this question from different angles, such as philosophy, psychology and science. People from these fields who heard about my book idea were immediately intrigued by the question it posed and I received contributions from Dr. Jonathan Miller, Liz MacRae Shaw and Professor Horace Barlow.

Jonathan Miller has written a foreword comparing the question I asked with the subject of an essay on consciousness by the philosopher Thomas Nagel. Professor Nagel invites the reader to consider the possibility that 'there is something it is like to be a bat'.

In the first epilogue, Liz MacRae Shaw, a psycho-dynamic counsellor, sees the personal reflections and descriptions of emotional states contained in this book as occupying a brand new landscape previously colonised by literature, therapy case studies and 'misery memoirs'.

'From early childhood we seek out stories, starting with our own,' she says. 'It is how we make sense of who we are.' Drawing parallels with Shakespeare's *Seven Ages of Man*, Mrs Shaw observes that despite difficult beginnings, many contributors have found a way to recover their psychological wellbeing through relationships, music and work, and she recognises the pleasure in reading about those who are similar to ourselves and yet so different.

In the final epilogue, Professor Horace Barlow, visual neuro-scientist and great-grandson of Charles Darwin, challenges the notion of where the benefits of introspection lie: not with the individual, he claims, but the community. Rene Descartes' revelation, 'I think therefore I am', 'messed us up', Professor Barlow says, giving introspection an unsavoury reputation and casting a 400 year spell. He explains that he thought through the question, 'What does it feel like to be me?' and concluded that the answer is not to be found by looking more closely at a single brain examining its own content. Instead, one has to view intro-spection in the light of the fact that *Homo sapiens* are a highly social species. We ask others why they did what they did and why they think what they think, and we not only expect reasonable answers when we ask these questions, but also expect to be able to reply with reasonable answers when asked these questions by others.

What Does it Feel Like to Be You?

I have asked this question of readers on the last page of the book. When I mention the idea of the book to people or they read some of its contents, the usual reaction is to attempt an answer. For instance, when Victoria, 20, sent me her piece, she added, 'It has been very interesting to write, but lots of my mates have expressed an interest, so if you need someone else of my age to write something I'm sure there would be lots of takers!'

My own doubt is that there is such a thing as 'Being a Self Forever', (John Updike's Chapter title), and recently a friend said his sense of identity is strong but without permanence: 'I see myself carrying a light that illuminates the wood, a bit ahead and a bit behind but the part behind is gone irretrievably.'

Jenny Salaman Manson

Zuky Serper

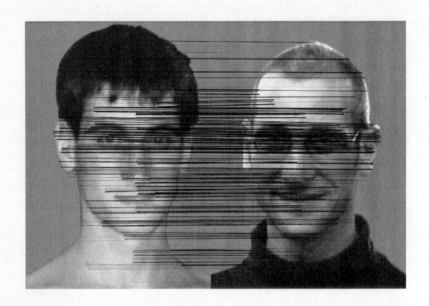

Two portraits: one from "there" and one from "here", fifteen years apart. The eye is running between the two, drawing a line from each point on the one to the other, trying to visualise and track the changes.

All the cells in a human body replace themselves every seven years. I read it somewhere a while ago. Does it mean that our self, that is, our bodily self, is reborn every seven years? So, is it the same being? Or a concept of continuity that is making us ourselves?

I came to England 10 years ago. There is not one cell in my body that experienced "first hand" my previous life in the sun, near the sea, working the land in the citrus orchard of my kibbutz, Sa'ar. I am all from here now. Or am I?

Foreword by Dr Jonathan Miller

In a legendary essay which bears a title similar to the one which Jenny Manson has chosen for this intriguing anthology of personal memoirs, the American philosopher, Thomas Nagel, invites the reader to consider the possibility that 'there is something it is like to be a bat'.

He argues that although it's impossible for human beings to imagine, let along know, what it's like to be sightlessly acquainted with the external world through the medium of echolocation, it seems reasonable to assume that since bats are living creatures as opposed to inanimate objects, they have a subjective experience of receiving and reacting to the organised echoes of the squeaks which they systematically broadcast into the world around them. In addition to efficiently steering their flight by such a method, they are, in some admittedly incommunicable way, conscious of what it is like to do so.

In other words, unlike Descartes, for whom animals were nothing more than 'brute machines' whose soullessness denied them the distinctively human privilege of being aware of their own existence, for Nagel and most of his contemporaries the now undeniable fact that animals and human beings are genetically related to one another by descent introduces the possibility that for each individual of the higher orders at least, there is something it is like to be one.

If there is, as Nagel claims, something it's like to be a bat, the chances are that it's like that for all bats of the same species. But it would a mistake to assume that the experience of being a particular bat includes the belief that other bats feel the same way. Because, although they are undeniably social creatures, insofar as they flock together and engage in mutual altruism, the extent to which each bat identifies itself as one of 'us bats' is altogether questionable. On the contrary, the co-operation I've just mentioned is achieved automatically without the participants being conscious of each other's existence.

But when it comes to human beings the situation is quite different, though not, as Descartes supposed, because we alone are blessed with ownership of an immaterial soul, but because the human nervous system has evolved to the point where it can support, for each individual, a voluminous consciousness, the communicable contents of which increase in complexity and versatility from one generation to the next. In contrast to other species, including those of our closest relatives, our mental capabilities amplify and deepen without any significant changes in our genetic makeup. Through the medium of imitation, emulation and explicit instruction, our concepts and capabilities have progressed to the point where they would be almost unintelligible to our human predecessors.

So how does this apply to the subject of this book? Well, for a start, the fact that human beings can express and convey to others 'what it's like to be me' is something which is denied to bats, because, although there is in all probability something it's like to be one, there is no way a bat can tell us what it's like. In fact, the absence of language which precludes the possibility of describing it to others diminishes the extent to which an individual bat represents it to himself, because, in the act of formulating the description of an experience, we find ourselves reconsidering what it was like, discovering aspects of it which hadn't previously occurred to us. 'Now I come to think of it, as I try to make it intelligible to someone else, what I saw, felt or heard, looks, feels and sounds somewhat different to how it originally seemed.'

And another thing: The desire to convey what an experience is like presupposes that the communicator recognises the existence of individuals sufficiently like himself to make it worth the effort of thinking out loud. And that is what bats can't do. Whatever it's like to be one, the experience, such as it is, does not include the knowledge of other individuals to whom the description would be interesting or even intelligible. So, with the exception of squeaking their way round the world, bats keep their traps shut.

But even if, by some inconceivable miracle, bats could tell us what it was like to be one, it's unlikely that we could distinguish one account from another, for the simple reason that the experience of being a bat is so simple that it leaves little room for individual, let alone describable, variation. In other words, listening to one bat you'd have heard them all. But as Jenny Manson's anthology shows, although they are recognisably accounts of what it's like to be *human*, to the point where each of them would be more or less intelligible to someone who lived five hundred years ago, there is no getting away from the fact that these personal accounts of 'What it feels like to be me' are sufficiently different from one another to be of interest to all of us.

PART I – SETTING OUT

(Ages 14-39)

Larry

To be Me

I'm not quite sure what that means. I guess the problem is I don't think about it very much. The unexamined life is not supposed to be worth living. I had always felt I did pretty well in that regard. I have always felt that I pondered life's questions more than most. As an introvert, I observe everyone else around me engaged in seemingly idle living, while I quietly observe and ponder the meaning of it all. Perhaps the truth is that I'm merely quiet. For, if I've spent all this time pondering things, surely I can answer a question regarding the essence of 'me'? But I cannot.

Am I the sum of my behaviour? Can one log my responses to stimuli to recreate me? Or are my thought patterns the real essence of me? If I were to write down the internal conversation taking place in my head every day, would that be enough for someone to know what it feels like to be me? Yet, how can someone understand me without also knowing my history, or my memories? All these things, however, can be seen as external to 'me'. My behaviours, my feelings, my memories, present themselves to the 'me' that responds to them.

So what then is left over that could make up 'me' when you subtract all these things? That's the real question isn't it? And I'm afraid I don't really ponder that question all that much. As a scientist, I don't have much patience for asking questions that, in my estimation, don't have answers. I haven't accepted the idea that getting the answer isn't the point. But that's part of 'me' I guess. The result of this characteristic has been a great difficulty in coming up with ideas for this project. Deciding what is mundane trivia unworthy of mention, or is a key theme needing examination, is difficult for me.

As a result, I've decided to just begin writing and see where things take me...

Perceptions of Me

I guess I'll start with a story that I often think back on. Back in my university days I played a game with a close group of friends which I found quite interesting. I've often wanted to play it again with contemporary friends. The game starts with everyone sitting down and forming a circle. Next, everyone pretends that the first person in the circle has left the room. Then, one by one, each person in the circle talks about that person. They can say whatever they want about that person. They can talk about how they feel about them, what is annoying about them, or what they think their future holds. The key is for everyone to try not to censor themselves. The person being spoken about is required to remain absolutely silent.

It would probably be very difficult to find enough close friends, with enough trust, and perhaps enough bravery to play a game like this now. We were all at university. For all of us, it was the first time away from home, and everything about life was new and exciting. We all were beginning to think about life in new ways. In this intense atmosphere, friendships form like none others in life I think. These are still my closest friends. On the night we played the game, in all likelihood we were enjoying another newly found interest, alcohol.

The thing I recall most about that night was the narcissistic pleasure of hearing, unfiltered, the perceptions my closest friends had of me. Who hasn't ever wanted to be a fly on the wall, overhearing conversations people were having about you? It was voyeuristic. I forget much that was said. The consensus among the group was that I was conservative in my ways. By this they meant that I didn't take chances in life, I played things safe and planned out my existence too carefully. I remember not very much liking to hear this. At the time I felt they were wrong.

I don't know when, but at some point in life I began to accept that this may indeed be a truth about me. While living life safely isn't the worst thing in the world, I saw it as something I wanted to change. It would be overly dramatic to say this was a watershed moment. However, the memory of this game is strong for me. I sometimes wonder if anyone else who played gives it a moment's thought. When I think about my life, and the decisions that I've made, I often construct the narrative to emphasise the risks that I've taken over the safe choices. It's as if I need to prove to myself and to others if they ask that I have indeed overcome this handicap. What about my risky job decisions, choosing small young companies, or my bravery in getting divorced, or my crazy leap across the Atlantic? Is that not proof that I'm a brave risk taker?

Memories

Why does the university circle game memory stick with me? I surely had experiences in university just as intimate, or just as exciting. For some reason the circle game for me is a memory which is easily and frequently recalled. The game is likely not remembered with the same passion by the other people present that night. It may be that two people could live absolutely parallel lives, yet retain completely different memories. For me, this is a most interesting fact about memory. What people instinctively remember is infinitely more interesting than the memories themselves. Why do people remember the things they do? What does it say about them? These, again, are questions I don't tend to ask or ponder.

I've been able to corroborate my first memory occurring when I was age four. I don't specifically remember being four; rather, my parents had determined I was four at the time in question. It's a very vague memory of being on vacation with my parents and some of their friends on Cape Cod. The specific memory is watching a play being put on by some of the older children in the back yard. To this day I'm not sure if this memory is real, or was implanted by subsequent discussions. Nothing evocative comes out of this memory; it is just my first. At or around the same time,

I remember being carried on my father's back while I was in fear of drowning. The area of Cape Cod where we were staying had tremendous tides. The tide had gone way out and we were digging for clams. I seem to recall bringing the clamming to an abrupt halt for my father, as I was afraid the tide would rush in and drown us.

It's hard for me to say what the most evocative memories of my childhood are. The most I can do is go through my personal biography and see what pops out. Until I was nine we lived in a small apartment. I recall those years as living in isolation. There were few children my age. The one friend I had was a little too old for me and dominated me. A few key events during those years in the apartment come easily to mind:

I would line up my small toy cars for a race. Then I'd move them all down the hall in formation to capture a freeze frame of the race up till that point. Then I'd move them again further down the hall, some cars now over taking others during that freeze frame. I'd keep doing this till the race was over.

I developed a love of throwing rocks. I was proud of my skill and strength. I soon learned that I could easily throw rocks over moving cars in the road. I was incensed when one of them stopped. The driver dragging me to my apartment so I could confess to what I was doing. I couldn't understand why no one appreciated the cars were never in danger because I was so skilled at throwing the rocks.

I had a friend or friends over one morning. At that age I was still not allowed to prepare food in the kitchen on my own. But as I wanted to impress my friend of my adulthood, I prepared our breakfast. As I was pouring the milk into his cereal, I spilled milk all over the place. In the commotion, my mother woke up and I was reminded in the strongest terms of the error of my ways.

One day in my first year class, I got in an argument with the teacher over the answer to the equation of 1×0. I was adamant that the answer was 0. She kept saying it was 1. It was about this time I began to realise that I had talent in the classroom. Moreover, I got the top grades in the whole class.

I can think of a few others during that time, but for brevity's sake I'll leave it at that.

When I was nine, my family moved to a house. It was in the same town, but was in a different school district. This was probably the most traumatic occurrence of my childhood. For whatever reason, I was not accepted by the majority of the children in the new school. I have many memories during the next four years. I'm uncertain which ones I would call most evocative:

- Being so afraid to go to school that I would nearly vomit in the mornings.

- Refusing to take on the class bully in a fight even when he offered to put one arm behind his back.

- During recess one day, the class bully demanded that everyone in the group utter a swear word. The best I could do was 'damn'.

- Voting for Ford during the mock class elections. Being teased because most of the other kids voted for Carter.

- Going to my first baseball practice and being told to go play right field (the place coaches put the least talented player), and having to admit I didn't know where that was.

- Getting one answer incorrect on a spelling test, denying me a perfect score, mostly because the teacher had a severe Boston accent essentially removing the letter 'r' from the word 'quarter'.

- Telling my sixth grade teacher I would do my book report on black holes. She asked me, 'What's a black hole?'

- Getting voted as 'Class Brain', and despite intense lobbying, coming in second as 'Class Clown'.

During these years, my social ineptness contrasted sharply with my academic prowess. Academia was a place where I could excel and was one of the few areas of my life where I felt confident. At the same time, I resented my academic skills to the extent that they kept me at a distance from everyone else. Eventually I moved up to high school, and began the complicated journey through adolescence. In the bigger school, I met people more on my academic and social level, and discovered girls...

Amelia

I have chosen to write about two areas of my internal life. The first section, titled 'Funny Feelings', describes a thinking process I went through as a child which involved, in retrospect, my coming to terms with the notion of dying. Secondly, I turn my attention to looking at myself in relation to others, including intimate others and the wider social world.

Funny Feelings

'Funny feelings' was the phrase of my seventh year. I had realised the strange notion of death and its inevitability, and this left me having frequent bouts of these feelings.

While it is quite amusing to look back on, at the time it was pretty horrible. These 'funny feelings' (FF) came over me like a big, heavy, dark cloak whenever left to myself or not absorbed in activity. I have the same difficulty describing FF now as I did then, as it was really an emotional state, probably what an adult would term feeling low or depressed. But I feel, and I did then, that this doesn't quite capture this FF business.

The most common time for me to be stricken by the FF was when playing with friends, usually when engaging in imaginary play. I had always found imaginative games far more exciting and absorbing than reality-based play, as what could compete with becoming a mum, baby, monster, teacher, goodie or baddie in one afternoon? I loved where such games would take me, such that I lost track of time, place and most importantly *me* during this time. Who could ask for more than being able to become older, wiser, more beautiful and more impressive all in an afternoon's play?

The trouble came when I hit about seven and a half. I was playing one of these fantastical imaginary games with some friends when I suddenly felt 'what is the point?' This feeling was a mixture between 'what is the point of this game/me playing in it?' and most alarmingly 'what is the point of the BIG game?' – namely life itself. As I have said, this was a horrible moment, an awakening of sorts which left me feeling emotionally winded and unable to continue with the game I was so engrossed in beforehand. I was no longer a player, one of the kids, absorbed in this wondrous different universe where I could be anyone. I felt like I had suddenly become an outsider, perhaps like an adult with the company of children, who had realised that play, like life, was effectively pretty meaningless. I finished the game with my friends, but felt that I was playing at playing.

Luckily, I felt I could confide in my mum about my new found FF. I think she was quite interested in this, as she has told me more recently. It became a frequent occurrence, in pace with my experience of this new state, that I took her aside to whisper, 'I have funny feelings.'

The tone of this message is pretty hard to convey in the written word, but it was like I was informing her of a revelation, not just that 'I was a bit upset'. FF to me had an extra gravitas, as they were not associated with a short-lived concern about the here and now but seemed to be something much bigger, at least to me. I was conscious then, as now, that at that age I should have been a bit lighter of heart and more concerned with who was my best friend that week, having the latest toy, excelling at the piano (not that I ever played) or the like.

At the same time as feeling pretty horrified that I was filling my mind with FF whenever I had free mind space, I suppose I have to admit I was also a little proud that I had such dark and, relatively speaking, mature/serious concerns while my peers concerned themselves with what I thought to be trifles. This may sound very arrogant now, but at the time I did feel my friends were missing the point. The flipside of the arrogance was the loneliness it presented, as it was difficult to realise my peers were concerned with matters totally other than the thoughts that were consuming me.

Again, I was really fortunate to have my mum who by now had become very used to my perpetual 'I have funny feelings', which had become 'I still have funny feelings' and then advanced into 'when will my funny feelings end?' I wanted my mum to offer me an idea of when these strange dark feelings would stop taking me over. I was very grateful that I did not have the less sensitive type of mother who might say, 'Quit this talk of FF and go and play' (i.e. get on with life and get immersed in the day to day like every other seven year old). But my mum could not solve this problem for me. She could and did understand what I was going through but she could not wave a magic wand and make the FFs disappear like she could help sort out a dispute with friends or a problem at school. This was a battle I would have to fight for myself, alone, and looking back, that was a pretty rude awakening. My mind, in a sense, was the enemy, and the battle was, therefore, only mine.

I remember so clearly when I tried to confide in one of my closest friends of the time about these FF. I thought that if I found that she too suffered from these I might not feel so alone. The friend I seized on to confide in (which I did in the back seat of the car when being driven home from school), was chosen because I felt she was sensitive and would not judge me badly for what I recognised was a bit of a strange worry. However, I clearly did not have the maturity to really convey to my friend what my FFs were, as when I told her about them and asked her if she got FFs, she said, 'Yes, sometimes, when my brother is annoying me'!

Because of my experience with this friend, and as I was conscious that this FF phenomenon was a bit strange for a seven year old, I kept this matter to myself apart from telling my mum. Thinking about it now, an adult would have probably been more capable of dealing with the FF business, as they would have the right language for it. I knew what I felt, but I lacked the world-liness and communication skills to be able to find much comfort from the outside world in this lonely stage. My mum later told me that I suffered from a childhood depression in coming to terms with death, which is funny to imagine (perhaps I should stop overusing this f word!). I guess she is right, but at the time, it felt like something no one else could possibly experience. Oh the egoism of childhood!

I did not only suffer the FF when playing, but also when doing things like shopping. When I had been younger, the process of purchasing had filled me with endless glee and I could not be taken to any retail outlet (be it a pharmacy, garden centre or any other unlikely shop) without trying to come away with a little something (what we now refer to as retail therapy). But this FF seemed to say to me in shops – 'What do you want these new things for? What is the point of them?' I can imagine my parents were pleased. I had become less of a pest in wanting to always spend money everywhere I went, but for me, it was quite a letdown not to get the thrill of the spend.

The FFs did gradually lift, both in severity and frequency, and lasted in total probably no more than a year or so, but while I have not suffered from depression as an adult, I get a whiff of these FFs from time to time. Usually, they hit when doing something which should be good fun, like shopping. I do still get the 'What is the point?' feelings sweeping over me (Christmas shopping/sales seem to be a typical trigger), but without the accompanying seismic emotional wave. Perhaps, on reflection, having had these concerns at a very early stage made me come to terms with the fact that, at least in my view, there is not a lot of point to most things we do in life. So the best tactic is joining the whole mad existence of humanity getting absorbed in the micro concerns of 'Do I want to go and see this film or that? Has so and so upset me? Should I get the 10am or 10.30am train?' and other matters of *vital* importance. They do say depressives are just realists. I would rather not be a realist in that case – delusion does me just fine in the battle to keep the FFs at bay!

Me and Others

I have a strong need to be very open with those close to me, and I am aware that I do not filter much of what goes on in my head before I communicate to my nearest and dearest. If there is a worry of the season, I share this with my husband/best friend/sister/mum/dad with very little concern for their interest in the obsession.

But what this does mean is that I tend not to feel lonely in life, as those nearest to me are only too aware of the meanderings of my mind. In fact, my husband often says in joke that he doesn't need to know about every little thought that pops into my head! And perhaps I am guilty of giving every mood/thought/idea too much weight.

I guess this is because of my temperament, but also because I hold the view that whatever people feel cannot be wrong or bad. As I don't knowingly judge people on what they feel, I assume my trusted others will do the same for me. All the feelings which we might think are dark – jealousy, envy, anger, introspection etc. – are, I guess, so natural and human, if a little bleak, that I feel everyone should be able to be open about them. I'm not sure the world is a cuddly enough place for everyone to be able to do this in the wider social context of work/college etc; but a feeling that people can be open with their closest group can only help our passage in life.

The result of this is that I do not feel the need to speak to someone outside my immediate support circle as a means of release. There is an upside to this because being open, while it can be disarming to others, can also be rather overwhelming and threatening to those with a very different style. I have made the mistake of over-exposing myself emotionally with those in a new job, which meant that I felt compromised for several months. But things did get better.

I am rarely offended by my closest confidantes. This I know must come in part from a better mutual understanding, but it is also the case that I like my husband, etc, to be very frank with me. I take his comments and those from people I am close to, both negative and positive, in a reasonably robust way as I know they are based on the right motives.

I can much more easily be upset by the words and actions of those in my wider social circle, be it at work or with acquaintances. I hate being misunderstood, and I think I expect too much of people really, as I assume that they should fully understand me. I also find it very difficult to handle when I feel people behave in what I consider to be an unreasonable manner to me or my friends/family. I can work myself into a frenzy of anger when this happens, which I recognise damages me and not the person whom I perceive as the offender.

What is clear to me is that central to my feelings of security in life are the close relationships I have. Those who enter my inner circle tend to stay there. Notably my best friend dates back to when we were four years old and I met my first serious boyfriend at university in 1997 who became my husband in 2005.

But there is one other side to all this: parties, etc, can offer me a real rush, as I enjoy banter and laughter offered by a larger group. But I am never under the illusion that this is what I need to feel okay about myself (although I can sometimes really benefit from being forced out of my head for a few hours when I socialise). I have noticed this with others too, that sometimes when you are worried about something it can be helpful to be at a party, as this removes the temptation of going into moan mode and putting on a good face can sometimes do the trick internally too.

Victoria

Getting to Know Myself

This is not something that I have ever thought about. To be honest, I know that I am still a very long way off knowing everything about myself, but this is what I know so far:

I am 20 years old. I was raised in the south of England to a fairly normal family. My parents separated when I was eight and me and my sister lived with my dad until I was seventeen when I moved out with my then boyfriend. I moved back in, with my mum this time, when I was eighteen. After a break from education I returned to college this year, and I currently live with my boyfriend and one flat mate. Looking back, the different periods of my life seem very separated. My teenage years were difficult (as everybody's are) and I don't really feel like I can relate too much that happened from the age of thirteen until about nineteen. At the moment though I feel very satisfied; standing on my own two feet has made me feel much more secure about everything, and my relationships with my family are better than they ever were. I am relieved that I can feel myself making progress after what feels like a long period of uncertainty.

My parents and my sister have obviously affected who I am. My mum and dad are the complete opposites of each other. Mum is arty and impulsive. I know that I could say absolutely anything without shocking her, but she is a bit mad sometimes. Dad is far more together and sensible. He is probably the more intellectual one of the pair. Although I have felt closer to my mum in the past, I am definitely more like my dad – we think in the same way.

I have one sister who is two and a half years younger than me, and we are typical siblings. We have got on better together over the last couple of years but when we do fight it only gets worse with age. I hope that there is a limit on this, and I know that we will remain very close, although I don't think we will ever be able to live together again without very serious rows.

I am a fairly shy person although this has got better recently. I don't know if I have become any more confident, or just started caring less what people think – a bit of both probably. I get frustrated because I know people think I am quiet and mousy, but it is often that I just can't find the right words when I am around new people, rather than that I don't want to talk.

I am a serial worrier. I think I get it from my dad: we are not very good at telling people how we feel so we worry about things instead. I don't think it's a problem – in fact, I'm generally a very positive person – it's just my way of dealing with the world. I always feel at a bit of a loose end if I don't have something to worry about.

These are my recent worries:

Making the Wrong Choices

I know how lucky I am to be able to choose how I want to live. It is partly because of this that I am so concerned about not wasting this by making bad choices. In the last few years I have been trying to work out what I want to do for a career, and I still have no idea. Although I would probably be happy doing more or less anything, I am very conscious that if I do find myself doing a job I don't enjoy it is only my fault – I cannot blame anyone else. I am also unsure of how to justify the choice. Should I be doing what makes me happy, or rich, or something that helps other people?

When I left school I went to art college because I thought at the time that this was what I wanted to do. Partly because I love anything creative and partly because my mum is the same and I know she really regrets not studying art further. I did not want to get old and wish I had done something I hadn't. In the end though I felt that I was being too self indulgent; art was a hobby really so it seemed like I was taking the easy option.

My views on what I 'should' do for a job are still very affected by my time at school. I went to a grammar school where pupils were only measured in terms of academic ability (I think running off to art school may have been a bit of a rebellion against this). I didn't do badly, sort of kept my head down and got on with it. I left after the first year of A levels, which is one of the best things I have done, otherwise I think I would have just got caught up in moving in a particular direction and not stopped to think about it until ten years down the line, which would be too late to change anything. As a result of the school, though, I set very high standards in terms of grades, etc. which means that I am quite hard on myself when I don't achieve them. I absolutely hate the idea of the school now, but I have a fondness for it, from spending so much time there I guess, which it is hard to shake off, however much I think I have grown out of it.

Luckily, all this thinking about the 'big' things does stop me getting caught up and dithering over the smaller ones. I'm generally quite rash when it comes to day to day decisions, which is good because I follow my instincts and haven't got any major regrets so far. An idea of roughly where I want to end up keeps me going in the right direction so I'm trusting that I will end up more or less where I want to in the end.

Unease

This is a very bad title but it's the closest I can think of for the occasional feelings that I get. I'm not in any way depressed about my life but I do occasionally get a sense of hopelessness, or things not being right with the world. It's a very small thing; it usually only lasts a couple of minutes, and it happens far less frequently as I get older. I don't really know how to describe it, apart from as a feeling of panic or unease in the bottom of my stomach. I don't think it's necessarily a bad thing, and I have learned to listen to it. If a person or a situation causes it then I put it down to my instincts telling me to stay away. I do get scared, however, when I feel it for no apparent reason as it's normally followed by something bad happening (last time I got it really badly my mum had a car crash), so if it happens I tend to lock myself in the house until I find out the cause.

Getting Old

It's not so much getting old that I'm scared of, as getting old without feeling any older or more prepared for life. I suppose I'm just going to have to get used to it, as I'm always being told that I won't ever feel any more grown up. But I was hoping that it would have all started to fall into place by now.

I also worry about my parents getting old. My little sister is about to leave home and I'm actually sort of concerned about whether they will be alright. I think that's one of very few things that would be better if they still lived together. Of course I know this is totally irrational, they were both fine before we were born and they probably can't wait for the peace and quiet.

Stephen

Stop the World

I stroll into my local newsagents, pick up a paper and have a humorous exchange with the shop assistant. 'Christ, I'm funny,' I think to myself. 'Someone should follow me around and film me. I'm on form. I feel great. My life is a work of art...' And it's true; I feel incredible, unstoppable, an irresistible force. 'You are the best, Stephen,' I say. 'You are *special.*' Yet these feelings have a flip side, and it's the flip side I have spent half my life trying to escape.

My earliest memory of consciousness is playing in the hallway of my childhood home. The sun is streaming through the stained glass of our front door and a thousand dust particles are disturbed by my activity. I am warm, safe and comfortable. Everything is rosy. But I stop. I realise that I am not happy, not happy at all. I am too young to understand anything of what I feel but I know something is wrong. I decide to swallow it down because I am ashamed of my feelings. I am five.

Growing up, the only emotion I can recall is fear, and all my memories swim in its presence. I am fearful of everything: swimming baths, trains, this teacher, that pupil, making mistakes and any kind of responsibility. I cannot handle being Reserve Overhead Projector Monitor at junior school, for instance. For those of you unsure, responsibility does not come much less demanding. Every morning I telephone the incumbent Overhead Project Monitor to check he's coming in. He does so every day except for one Monday. On that day I beam the words to *If I had a Hammer* upside down to the whole school.

My elderly father, almost 60 when I enter the world, combines a soft heart and great humanity with a ferocious temper. He explodes for no apparent reason and I am absolutely terrified of him. Although I am only a child I can see he is not a reasonable person. Much of my early life is spent hanging off the banisters listening to my parents argue. I wait for the right moment to intervene. 'Are things calming down?' I ask myself. They almost never are. Unable to bear it any longer, I dash downstairs and plead with my mother to stop goading my volatile father. This happens at least once a day and dominates the landscape of my childhood.

I have an awareness that in material terms my life is easy. Despite his temper my generous and loving dad invariably offers to buy me a gift on his regular trips into town. From a very young age I say 'no' because I sense that 'yes' will do me no good in the longer term. I know that I want my life to be harder, that I need more knocks, knocks that perhaps I would be receiving if I had siblings.

My father is a gifted, renowned journalist and he is very keen that I read. This I do with great pleasure, lapping up everything from *The Famous Five* and *The Beano* to labels on shampoo bottles. Yet the more I read, the more he forces me down certain literary corridors. My reading loses its freedom, slows up and finally grinds to a halt. This causes a terrible strain between us. By the age of nine I have devised a plan: when we are alone together I will talk to him constantly, filling the airwaves with anything I can think of in the hope that he will never find a moment to confront me about my lack of reading. I hate having a time bomb for a father and when it is just the two of us I will do anything I can to prevent his thunderous temper from surfacing.

This morning I lay pointlessly in bed. Like my dad I am a journalist. Like him I work mainly from home. 'What are you doing?' I say, chastising myself. 'You are 33 and you think it's fine to laze around on a Tuesday morning? How do you expect to prove you are this brilliant person you imagine yourself to be, to create a body of work that you are proud of, simply by lying here?' I begin a countdown from ten to zero. I will rise at zero. When I get to zero, a new countdown begins, from twenty…

At senior school, despite being a very promising rugby player, I am petrified of the game. I often feign illness before matches, choosing instead to stay home with my parents. Through the power of the mind I convince myself that I am unwell and begin to feel unwell as a result. In my second year I miss the first game of the season and in the second I break my leg badly. I spend my teenage years convinced that I have brought this upon myself, that I have 'abused' my talent. And I am fixated on the pain of the injury.

Two years prior to this my father has a heart attack. A year after my accident my mother develops cancer. Both recover. I wish that my father had died, though I barely acknowledge this thought.

As a teenager I rarely have trouble sleeping but on the occasions I do, and I come to count sheep, they are crazy, out of control. My imagination, it seems, is forever getting the better of me. I am frightened by my inability to control the sheep. They turn on me, morphing into distorted beasts, rampaging through my thoughts.

This afternoon I took a walk around my neighbourhood. Shamelessly I peer in through every window. I gaze at the people inside, extrapolate the facade, imagine, in fact, what it is like to be them. I am drawn to the rougher parts of my locale and do this regularly as a form of self-intimidation: 'Stephen,' I say to myself, 'If you do not push on, work hard, harder than you are currently working, you will end up here. Or worse. Look. Use your eyes. Is this what you want?' I have a recurrent anxiety that I will find myself washed up, broken down, loveless and homeless, drinking my life away in some fleapit or other.

I am galvanised into action and return home to begin work on this essay. Forever the procrastinator, I decide to sort through my clothes. It is shameful; almost everything I own – clothes, house, car – has a hole in it. I am scratching around just like my father did when he was my age. I consider the ways in which we resemble one another. I have a temper, though it presents itself very rarely and when it does can be accompanied by tears. I am amazed, as I write this, that I am now engaged in the same approximate occupation as him; he a literary critic, me a columnist and feature writer. He may have been a journalist but he had another role for which he was just as well-known amongst his peers, that of 'injustice collector'; seeking out and inevitably finding the slights and put-downs necessary to fuel his fire and reconfirm the view of himself as underdog. We are both natural outsiders, I muse, and tick another box. He once said to me, humorously, 'I am not a control freak, I am just here to control all the other control freaks.' We are not so different, I surmise. But there is one difference: unlike my parents, I am utterly determined not to underachieve. My father threatened, often verbally, to write the novel of the century, but suffered from writer's block. My mother, brighter even than he, was by her own admission 'frightened of the world'. Both promised much yet delivered little relative to their potential. I do not understand where my self-belief comes from but it has a power that can, on occasion, barely be contained as it burns itself to the surface, appearing as unshakeable confidence, even arrogance. Sometimes I have to fight hard to suppress the latter. And despite my current impoverished state I am not overly concerned for I have a rich seam of inner resource and a mind full of ideas that should carry me through.

1986. I am 13, brushing my teeth and staring up at the dusty shelf on which my parents soak their false ones. If Manchester wins their bid for the 1992 Olympics, I ponder, I will be nineteen when they roll around. 'Nineteen? Oh Jesus, how could I ever be nineteen? I'm too scared to be nineteen. I don't want to grow up – how can I grow up, I don't know how to?'

My parents enjoy having a child around the house and I don't want to hurt their feelings so I stunt myself, half-knowingly, for their advancing years. In binding my own feet, so to speak, I am complicit in an act of emotional arrested development. I refuse to acknowledge my awareness of the inherent wrongness in what I am doing because I have no idea of the future damage I am inflicting upon myself.

In my early-teens I transfer my sporting affections to cricket. I practice in the nets most evenings and read all there is to read on the subject. Cricket becomes my life. There is no room for anything else, certainly no room for thoughts. When I go to bed I think only of shots I have played, balls I have bowled, averages, statistics, Len Hutton 364, 1938 The Oval, Jim Laker 19-90, 1956 Old Trafford. I think about little else. I am burying the reality of my emotions deep within myself, though I feel a distant storm brewing.

Though I would dearly love to have hair on my legs like some of the other boys, I am fairly content with my physical appearance. That is until one lunch break when I overhear two older pupils talking about my girlfriend:

'Susan? You know Susan – she's going out with Stephen, the guy with the *big nose*.'

From that moment I take to looking at my nose in car windows, shops windows and, when at home, two mirrors at once. I am becoming more self-aware and more self-conscious.

I am a reasonable student but as I join the sixth form I enter what my mother would later call my 'vague' phase. My 'vagueness' is a manifestation of my fear of moving forward and no one can see it or say it, least of all me.

The process of writing this piece has already been painful; recollections of the past bringing excruciating memories. Often, when my thoughts are unbearable or lead to discomfort I will soothe myself with the involuntary arrival of guitar chords in my mind's eye. The chords are invariably minor and their appearance act as a palliative, killing the pain of the present and removing me from the source of anguish. Alternatively, I will be comforted by spontaneous childhood images; a bluebell-filled wood I used to stroll through, a pathway I would amble along, corners I would peer round. Sometimes I recall the shape of the words on the back of the same postcard that sat for years untouched in our kitchen.

My seventeen-year-old self is lying in the bath reading the newspaper. I realise that I cannot concentrate. I am becoming fearful of my own thoughts, thoughts surrounding the excitement and anxiety of sex, the future and of going to university. I am concerned that whilst all my contemporaries seem excited about this next step in their lives, I cannot bring myself to even talk about it. I take to doing the washing-up with my Walkman on and wear it everywhere I go. My dad, who by now I am engaged with in sporadic conflict, questions why I need to do this. He recognises, perhaps, that I am blocking out difficult thoughts, something at which I am becoming increasingly adept. Despite my underlying concerns, I am also increasingly aware of my knack at making people laugh.

At eighteen I am besotted with a girl called Nikki, a girl who is not besotted with me. I work hard to win Nikki's affections, harder than I have ever worked at anything. Eventually we pair up at a school disco but by now I do not know whether I even want her. I 'plan' a gap year between school and university. I do this because I am not ready to grow up and face the world. When people ask me what I'm going to do in my year out I tell them that I'm going to have a very long bath. When they've stopped laughing I change the subject.

My parents expect me to go to university. They went; everyone else is going, so presumably I have to, then? I contract glandular fever during the summer of my exams, flunk and scrape into university for the following year thanks to a generous letter from the school.

Nikki goes off to university and comes back one weekend to see me. I tell her that I am attracted to other girls and as I say these words what I can only describe as a black veil envelops me.

I am in a state of panic. I visit her in Sheffield two weeks later and we break up. I start drinking on my own and writing poetry. Still living at home, I can feel my father's advancing years seeping into me. I should leave but I do not have the inner resources. I fly to Israel and visit distant relatives. I write a poem entitled *Ugly*. I feel peculiar abroad and do not understand why. It was not even my idea to go. I return and tell everyone I had a great time, which is a lie. I am lying to everyone including myself. As my departure day for university beckons I feel increasingly frightened, frozen and rigid. I am withdrawing and unable to engage properly with anyone, though I maintain the pretence of normality. The day before I am due to depart I spend ten hours playing the guitar. That evening I meet my friends at the pub. They come back to my house and I have a panic attack. I ask them to leave and shut the front door. I realise that I am never going to be the same again.

If this collection is a study of consciousness, then the experience of suffering a nervous breakdown is clearly a very valid one since breakdown is a sickness of consciousness, a slow death from the inside out. In his book, *Malignant Sadness*, Professor Lewis Wolpert describes his own depressive breakdown. His introduction begins, 'It was the worst experience of my life. More terrible even than watching my wife die of cancer.' Though some may find this bewildering, even disturbing, for me it is an understandable and even rational reaction to an experience so terrifying, so extreme, so unutterably *different*, that it fundamentally defies accurate description or the possibility of passing on its true nature to the unencumbered. During my breakdown I would regularly fantasise about losing a finger, a hand, even a whole arm, just to be 'normal' again, for a year, a month, a week even. After a while I forgot what it was like to be 'normal'. Perhaps I never was 'normal'.

That day, the day before I went off to university, is one I have played out many times since. If only I had been able to talk to my mum about how I was feeling. If only I had said that *no, I wasn't going to university.* When I awoke the next morning, for an instant I felt normal, only for 'it' to come flooding back. Outwardly I would appear to be me, if a little nervy, but inside I was completely different to the person I had been just hours before. I understood instinctively that something extremely profound had happened to me though I didn't understand what it was. What I did know was that I could not express it, to my parents, to anyone. I was utterly ashamed of my feelings.

Arriving at university I said goodbye to my parents, unpacked my belongings, stacked my CDs and put some music on. All normal activities, though I was just going through the motions. Something extraneous had entered me, a malignant presence. If only I could get at it, isolate it and siphon it off, then I would be fine. I *am* fine, except for this *thing*. All I need to know is *what is the matter with me?* Just give me a name. I have to know.

I steal into the medical bookshop and sneak a read about panic:

'Panic attacks take two to three months to recover from.'

'Two to three months? There is no conceivable way that I will 'recover' in that time. I am stuck like this. This is how I am now. Whatever it may say in the book, it is inconceivable that I will ever recover from this.'

What it felt like to be me at this time was alarming: I was agitated, panicky, distressed, deeply confused and in a state of shock. To compound matters I was hiding all of this behind a wisecracking autopilot. My life was on fire, my situation seemingly irretrievable, insoluble and intolerable. My mind continued as it had done since I suffered my first panic, haring around in circles, searching for an answer, endlessly repeating the same patterns. Yet, at the same time, I could not think beyond the fact that I could think. And I thought, continuously.

As the breakdown takes hold, my first few weeks at university are hell. I lie in bed in the mornings torturing myself with anxious thoughts so intense that after a few minutes I run to the bathroom and vomit. My appetite has completely disappeared except when I am drinking. Alcohol is the only thing that brings me relief from myself through a blotting of consciousness and reduction of anxiety. In fact booze is the only leading post that helps cut through my layers of fear and reminds me of the person I used to be. Every cell in my body is screaming. The nerve endings on the skin of my stomach are especially sensitive, so sensitive that my stomach is too tender to have clothes touching it. Much of my time on campus is spent with my hand between my shirt and my burning skin. I smoke drugs because other people are doing it. It induces several panic attacks, some of which last for hours. I visit my doctor and start taking anti-depressants. All the while I am stuck in the very place, university, that triggered these feelings, though by now my existence cares little for the external. The maelstrom is within, not without.

Company and alcohol are my only escape. The pub is my most comfortable environment, though a trip to the bathroom will invariably follow a set pattern:

'How do I look? Can people see how damaged I am? Can they tell that I am desperate? They must be able to. Surely they can see it in my eyes? *I* can see it in my eyes. Maybe I should wear dark glasses? Perhaps I can have plastic surgery, to make the corners of my mouth turn upwards, so I don't have to try and seem happy all the time. No one must know I am anything other than happy.'

The only part of myself that seems to have remained intact is my sense of humour. Coming naturally to me, it is the only way I can deal with the world whilst keeping it at bay.

One morning during the second term I wake rigid and cannot move. Eventually hauling myself up, I concoct a story about my grandfather being ill and flee. Once home I unravel before my father. He is distressed and confused. One quarter-recovered, I return a week later. I spend most of my university career in a perpetual cycle, lurching from one obsessional fear to another, by turns terrified of crowds, being alone with one person, blushing during tutorials, vomiting during lectures, sweating and so on. I do, however, start seeing a counsellor on campus. Somehow I make it through university though I leave with no notion whatsoever of a 'career'. 'How can I?' I tell myself. 'I am holding on, seeing my friends. That's all I can do.' Truth be told, my mind had always been paralysed by fear, certainly too scared to consider the future. My malaise was one of progress. My sickness was in being thrust headlong into a future for which I had no resources to cope. Time was making me unwell. I needed it to stop, or reverse.

After graduating, I move in with a cousin and busk for a living, but I get a recurrence of glandular fever, become extremely anxious and return home. I start temping and after a year fall into sales, a job that, as an anxious young man living off the now-distant memory of what it is to be confident, I am ill-equipped to undertake. My parents relocate to Wales and I move in with my grandmother in London. Within a year my mother is diagnosed with secondary cancer and is given a year to live. I drive home and get caught speeding. I visit my mother in hospital in Wales. That evening I go for a run and have a panic attack that leaves me panting and immobile by the side of the road. I go back onto anti-depressants and my spirits pick up a little. I am not a natural salesman but I do well enough at my job. My mother's prognosis is improved, yet just when she is getting back on her feet my father dies of a heart attack. Now I must bare the brunt of my mother's illness.

By this point I have *been this way* for six years and have more or less accepted it as my lot. My overall mood can be lifted by medication but there is still something fundamentally wrong. My mind is not under my control. I have learnt to live in a small, taut world that bears little resemblance to my previous existence. I have a career that is meaningless to me and I am fearful of promotion. I have also learnt to cut out, to sever myself from myself. This is a blessing: self-examination is minimised as I fall into the deepest sleep the moment I crawl into bed. This ability to cut out is especially acute when I'm driving, leading me to pull over many times, often less than a mile from home, to find instant sleep.

I have a string of girlfriends. I feel anxious and uncomfortable around them, especially the ones I find most attractive. I dare not reveal the full extent of my true self. I won't allow anyone to get close to me, feeling more comfortable with seductions and brief romantic forays than sustained relationships.

Despite my best efforts I am promoted. At the same time, as my mother lies in hospital, I have to sell the house in Wales. I go under, am not coping at all. I cannot bear to be me. I keep counting the years since my first panic attack. 'How long have I been like this?' After years of counselling, I begin seeing a psychotherapist three times a week. Unable to confront my own problems, I am paying someone a minor fortune to think with me. For the fifty minutes we are together I will focus absolutely on my difficulties. When I leave, I will not consider them again until we reconvene. When we do, I never remember what we were talking about previously.

Time again heals me back to some sort of normality. Feeling a little better in myself, my promotion is a success and I surprise myself by thriving on the responsibility. At the end of the year I am offered a different role, a promotion again. I take it and, coinciding with rejection from the first woman I genuinely open up to, I truly collapse within myself. I ring my doctor and ask him how easy it is to be admitted to The Priory. He tells me not very easy. I struggle on, and somehow do not miss a day of work, though I am sure it is clear to all that I am ill. But I begin to recover. And just as I free myself from my winter-time collapse, I am made redundant, and my mother dies, in the space of three weeks. It is 2001 and I am twenty eight.

I grew up with a strong sense of my dad's mortality, though

far less so my mum's. I used to get very scared when dad and I travelled somewhere on our own together, frightened that he would have a heart attack in front of me. My mother, on the other hand, I had no concerns about until I was 13. After that did I realise that they were both on borrowed time? Possibly. Did it affect me? Probably. Truth be told, any fear of separation was inbuilt from a very early age. I can recall as clear as yesterday an experience with my father when I was about six. We were in the local newsagents. This was a tiny shop but at the time it felt like a cave. We would often go together to purchase a bundle of newspapers, plus cigarettes for my dad. On this occasion I lost him as he browsed. In that instant I thought I would never see him again and became frantic. I recall the incident often. This, I am sure, did not bring about a fear of abandonment but was instead a manifestation. Believe it or not, to this day I cannot remain in a shop for long without seeking out the person I'm there with.

The death of my parents, especially my mum, was of course very painful. Yet death is a hefty dose of reality and since much of what I was experiencing was more in my head than in the world, to focus on an external reality rather than a spectral shadow was, in a small way, a relief. To paraphrase Wolpert, to be sad is preferable to being depressed.

I would never have wanted it this way, but my mother's death in particular led to a large outpouring of love and affection from almost everyone I knew. On the day of my mother's funeral, as we all stood outside staring at the wreaths after the service, I broke down. The party seemed to encircle me, as if I were the bud of a flower and they the petals and I was held together by a sea of bodies. I have never felt as loved as I did in that moment and this sustained me for quite some months...

After the death of my mother I move in with an overseas friend. I drink too much and wet the bed. I squander my inheritance. I begin writing a novel and start an affair with a lesbian. I return home and date a woman four years my senior. Freed from the pressures of work and protected by an apparently endless money blanket, I relax and think clearly for the first time about what it is that I am going to do with my life. I toy with a career in advertising but eventually take on a sales role in central London. Almost immediately I struggle, go under and resign to my manager in a local café. He suggests I see how I feel after the weekend.

I work as a Samaritan and that Sunday night I receive the most harrowing call I could possibly imagine. Although I am writing this under a pseudonym I am still not at liberty to say, but it involves the death of two people. I handle it well and it gives me confidence. I retract my resignation. I find that I am able to cope better at work. I develop a thicker skin and my team produces excellent results. I am *the man*, a success, making lots of money. I am promoted again, and again, and finally into a senior role for which I have no experience. My inability to cope creeps up on me but when it finally gets me, it takes me down. I start taking pain killers in an attempt to manage my feelings. I visit the Managing Director and, unable to look her in the eye, resign from my job 'to write a novel', which is a lie.

I am home now, and suicidal. I still have a little money left, enough to live on for a year or two, but I feel without resource. Just like mothers and their memories of the pain of childbirth, I am barely able to recall my thoughts and feelings from this time. My therapy has, it seems, been of little use. My girlfriend moves in to the flat I bought the year before. I am so depressed and broken that I want to die. I write in my diary that I am scared I will, almost unbeknownst to myself, commit suicide. I cannot hold a thought in my head, forget everything, leave keys in locks, doors open, milk in the oven, tea in the fridge. Despite all of this I decide that I am fed up with taking anti-depressants so wean myself off them. I try to write but nothing interesting or meaningful comes, partly because I am too ashamed to draw on my own personal experiences as a framework.

I am lying in bed on New Year's Day night. I am slightly on the mend, but feeling very delicate, and totally unsure about what life holds for me.

'Just relax, Stephen,' I say to myself. 'Nothing is going to come to you if you are tense. Just try and relax, and see what happens...'

Then something miraculous happens: I have what I regard as a great idea for a book, a phenomenally great idea for a book. It comes almost fully-formed. I get up and write down everything that I can think of related to this idea. I go back to bed. I have more ideas. I get up again. I go back to bed. I have more ideas but don't want to disturb my girlfriend so I write them down, in the dark, on paper I cannot see, hoping I will be able to read them in the morning.

Though a non-believer, this event has an almost spiritual quality to it. Overnight my crippling anxiety dissolves. I have a project and something to focus my mind on. I write solidly for four months. I start having 'normal' feelings and reactions. My girlfriend breaks up with me. I know it is for the best and I feel 'normal' about it. 'Normal' thoughts and feelings – what a joy! I realise that what I am experiencing is happiness. I begin to daydream, to see my name up in lights. I do not recall having ever daydreamt before. After two more brief sojourns into the world of sales I get lucky and am offered regular commissions for a magazine publishing house...

It would have been impossible for me to write this composition without giving a central role to my protracted breakdown. It is something that has been, for me, almost impossible to talk about all these years and I am grateful for the opportunity to do so. Of course many people suffer some kind of collapse in their lives and in some respects mine spared me the acuteness that others suffer: I never had to go to hospital, for instance. I know that my experience was not unique. It was, however, unique to me. What I found so terrifying was the absolute certainty that I was *stuck like this*. I had little reason to believe otherwise since I had felt this way constantly for almost twelve years. Terrifying, too, that I was not the master of my own mind and that in all that time scarcely an ordinary thought entered my head. I confided in almost no one, and lived two lives: one that continued, day-to-day, with work, friends, girlfriends, and another, private life that rendered the first life redundant.

Was I actively suicidal? No. When I felt this way, briefly, it was merely the workings of a mind scanning for the nearest exit rather than the detailed scheming of the truly defeated. In the end my life force, allied to my curiosity, were strong enough to keep me going.

My book is currently on the back burner but I have various other projects on the go. Despite the seriousness of this piece – or perhaps because of it – I have a feeling my future may lie in comedy writing (a 'funny' feeling, if you like). Where once I cowered at the future's looming presence, and fear drove me down into myself, furrowed my brow, bowed my back and fizzed my mind, that same future now excites me. I am so excited, in fact, that I fear one last trick will be played on me: that I will die young and not have the opportunity, finally presented to me, to fulfil my potential. For the first time life feels precious.

Despite this notion of 'before' and 'after', it would be wrong of me to suggest that I am out of the woods. I continue to drink too much. An especially alcohol-fuelled night leads to extreme anxiety and a fear that I have stabbed someone (I haven't). I realise that I must cut back on my drinking or run the risk of ruining my mental health. At the time of writing, I feel as if it is under control. If I lose control once more, I will stop drinking for good. That's the plan anyway.

I enjoy my own company, though there are still occasions when I struggle to be with myself, become frightened by my own thoughts and worry that I am slipping back. Clearly anxiety is part of who I am. Occasionally, I ruminate that this anxiety was handed down as the result of a childhood trauma suffered by my grandmother, which she passed onto her daughter – my mother – and my mother onto me. It makes me feel better but it is probably only half the truth. More pertinent is that I am who I am and this is what I must deal with. Indeed since my 'recovery', I have had three longish bout of anxious thinking, where I have been thrust back into my previous state. Clearly there is some kind of pattern to my periods of sickness and health. My challenge is in managing the periods of sickness, to the point where their effect is less noticeable. Early on, during the writing of this piece, I was struck down by an attack of anxiety lasting two weeks, where all I could think about was *this thing that was back*. It was brought on by an over-zealous reading of my diaries from my early twenties for the purpose of this composition. I thought I would be fine, hardened to it all now, imagined the writing of this essay to be a breeze, and silently mocked those who I knew had been offered the chance to contribute, but declined. It is amazing, on occasion, how unknowable our reactions can be.

Due to my relative and recent renaissance, I am outgrowing some of my friends. I want them to see the changes in me but they continue to pigeonhole, painting me as the clown or drunken oaf. I am no longer that person: I am quieter, more refined, soberer, leaner like my adolescent self and *happier*. I need very little in my life, which is just as well. I have almost every-thing I need for now, though I do want more – certainly in terms of achievement and career.

There is a couple with a young child downstairs from me. He is blonde, engaging and can almost say my name. I want to be a father. I long for my own children. Perhaps I will have children with my new girlfriend. We are getting on that well. My heart is more open than it has ever been.

But the truth of the matter is that I am scared about my

capacity to love. I have a strong desire to stay the course with her, but I worry that I will not be able to see it through, with her, with anyone. I get scared, find closeness very hard to handle, feel claustrophobic and want to cut and run. Naturally, I wish to free myself from this pattern. I am worried and embarrassed by my inability to endure a lasting relationship. I hate being like this, still do not fully understand it, but am determined to resolve it once and for all.

Often I think myself too brilliant, occasionally the opposite. It is an ongoing struggle and I oscillate wildly. Am I special? I know I should say 'no' but I can't bring myself to. Not yet, anyway. Whether it's true or not, the fact that I think it has certainly helped me at times in my life. This notion of my being 'special' was the soundtrack to my childhood. These days it acts as a kind of defence. But defences, masks and props can sometimes serve a vital purpose. To that end I would like to raise a toast to an old friend of mine: alcohol. Though it does me little good these days, in the early stages of my breakdown it helped remind me that the old me was still lurking somewhere beneath the surface. Without it, life would have been impossibly bleak. So here's to you, Mrs Alcohol.

I still do not know entirely what it is I should be doing: writing, playing music, performing or perhaps something else entirely. I guess I will find out. Maybe I have already, I don't know. What I *do* know is that I am happier than I have ever been. It seems that I have finally found direction and that has made all the difference. Reading this back, I realise that I have been given a second chance.

My father found some kind of fame, and certainly his fortune, in a collection very similar to this one, propelling him as it did from his hermitic broken-down life of poverty and obscurity and into the mainstream. I ponder whether I will be 'discovered' in a similar manner. I think not. I do not have his talent. Nor, to his eternal *chagrin*, am I well-read. Still, I conclude that I need not rely on being 'discovered' since I know that I will get to where I need to, in the end.

Where I live there are a number of blue English heritage plaques. My ambition is to have one of my own. Considering my only desire for so many years was to feel normal, I say why not?

Postscript

In the months since writing this essay, life has encompassed the best and worst of times. I'll settle for that. Better to have loved and lost. I have loved and embraced life, lost this love, then found it again. As for romantic love, that's another essay, novel or mini-series.

Re-reading my essay I am struck at how serious and, well, *earnest* I seem, and also how biography appears to take precedent over the central question. Perhaps I didn't have the energy for both. Perhaps I felt that to outline one was to explain the other. Maybe I just wanted to tell my story. It's a rather dramatic story, too. Melodramatic? Perhaps. It's not that the story wasn't true, but it could have been told from a different, less self-absorbed standpoint. But then again, if you asked me the question, 'What is it like to be you, Stephen?' one of the answers would certainly be 'self-absorbed'.

I remain a secret fuck-up, though not quite as secret as I used to be. I would hate to be defined by any aspect of myself, especially since these days *it* comes and goes less frequently, even though it is never absent. This essay, though, remains up my sleeve. I could unleash it into my world of friends and family and my life would never be the same again, probably in a good way. It's true that I'm getting pretty tired of putting on a front. In an instant I could explain away all the awkwardness, inconsistency, all the times 'you' have felt unable to connect with me. I'm not sure if I'm ready for that, but I may yet be tempted. For now it's enough to tell you that my name isn't Stephen.

Nina

What I Know So Far

Since I am only 14 years old I am still learning about what it feels like to be me. This is what I know so far:

I have moved around quite a lot during childhood, from Oxford to Israel to London to Belgium and back to London again. This, until recently, left me with a relatively confused identity. I knew I was English but had no obvious attachment to England whilst I was living in Belgium. All I had in London was a house, and some fading memories. Coming back to London as an older child meant I had, and still have, the ability to explore it and get to know where I live better. This has helped me develop a real sense of identity. I feel fond of Hampstead Heath and proud to live in proximity to exciting places in central London. I also like telling my friends from Belgium about the amazing city I live in! Having a place I can call home makes me feel much more confident and happy.

As a child, one of the things which seems most important is school. I have had many mixed experiences with my various schools. What adults do not always understand is that since most of a child's life is spent at school, they really have to like it or their entire life becomes difficult. This was certainly how I felt when I moved back to England at 13. I was shy, I was nervous and I was terribly worried about what people thought of me. The first few months at my private, competitive girls' school were really horrible. It felt like a boot camp compared to my easy-going mixed school in Belgium. Suddenly I had to really work in lessons – I couldn't just coast along. I had always taken my relative intelligence for granted; suddenly there was so much I didn't know, academically and socially. I felt hugely self-conscious and tongue-tied around schoolgirls who all knew each other already. I only knew one or two girls at the beginning, whom I thought I liked but they were actually keen to disown me as soon as I had some trouble settling in. Everything I said seemed ridiculous and I knew people were getting the wrong impression of me. I felt really unhappy as in Belgium I had had a close group of friends and now I felt so alone.

Gradually, I formed a circle of friends and went on a school trip to Germany. When I came back, I had a few good friends and now, a year later, I have a large group of people who are my friends. I feel I have learnt a lot from the experience of being new; it isn't easy, but if you don't make an effort to make friends, you never will.

I have recently discovered that I do have an intellectual side, or at least that I enjoy learning. Since I developed my French whilst living in Belgium, I was ahead when I came back to England and I now pursue this subject quite keenly. I like being told that I am the best at something; it's definitely an ego boost! It is also pleasing to know that my efforts are being noticed. I never really thought that school could be rewarding and thought of it as a compulsory place which I would leave as soon as I could. I am also interested in History and Politics. I have learnt to follow current affairs and this makes me feel more involved with the world and what is going on around me, as when I was younger I had my head in the clouds most of the time. People still seem surprised when they find me concentrating intensely on something, which gives me an indication of what a short attention span I must have had a few years ago. In fact, when I was listening carefully to a speaker who came to my school, I was told that I looked 'a bit depressed', when in fact I was just trying to keep up with complicated vocabulary. I think people are still discovering the fact that I do have a side of me that wants to learn!

Another side of me which I think is still developing is my religious and spiritual belief. I am Jewish, but in Belgium there was a relatively small and mostly American community. I never really felt comfortable with my faith, as none of my friends were Jewish. I preferred to think of myself as 'neutral' and even found the fact that I belonged to a seemingly obscure religion vaguely embarrassing. London, particularly the area in which I live, has a larger Jewish population. Suddenly lots of people around me were Jews just like I was, and I felt interested to learn more about who I was. There was a huge part of my identity which I had discarded for so long. I have generally made friends with people who are not religious and I have not become particularly observant. I just liked discovering that there was a whole group which I could be part of. I decided to have a late *Bat Mitzvah* to fit properly into the community (and to get lots of presents). It was a really fun experience and it was good to understand things which had never made sense to me before.

Many people describe me as a happy person, and I also think that I am an optimist. However, it is not that simple to categorise me. Although I do try to look on the bright side, I sometimes feel depressed if I have too much work or have been arguing with my friends or family. I am normally able to express how I feel easily but if I am upset I can end up feeling lonely. I don't stay moody for very long though. I realise that I am very lucky in my life, and there is no point getting upset about petty things when there are so many worse things in the world. Even if I do start sulking about unimportant things, I try to think about other people whose lives are much worse than mine and I realise that I should just be happy with who I am.

I feel more confident when I am with other people, but I do try to be comfortable in my own skin. My own appearance is important to me and I do feel better when I look better, although a proverb I strongly believe in is 'it's what's on the inside that counts'. I might have not made friends with someone a few years ago unless they were attractive, but there is so much more to people. I have also realised that people who are shallow are probably unhappy.

When I first meet people, I do not think that I am as friendly as I could be, as I am quite shy at a first encounter. However, once I get to know a person I think they see me as I am. My friends think that I am generally cheerful, friendly and funny and I agree. But people do not always understand me fully as my personality is quite complicated! I think that my self-esteem is much higher than it used to be and this helps me make friends. I used to regret a lot of things which I did and constantly tried to change my personality and the way I interacted with other people, probably just to look cool now that I think about it! I still care about how other people see me but I try to just be nice to people and hope that they will see the real me, and gradually get to know me better.

For the future, I have the same hopes as most people; for my family and me to have a happy life. I would like to do well at school and go to a good university, and then I have my whole life ahead of me to make other decisions. Although the idea of becoming an adult is intimidating, it is also exciting and I hope that it will be a great journey.

Peter Phillips

Butterflies

This poem was inspired by a challenge to me and fellow poets at a workshop to write about masturbation, which was something I neither wanted nor thought I would be able to write about.

It took quite a bit of consideration, but it came down to finding a suitable metaphor, and once I realised how I could describe the sense and feeling of first sexual arousal, and ensuing mixed feelings of excitement and guilt, the poem almost wrote itself – it was all done with butterflies.

Bath Time Butterflies at Boarding School

A white butterfly comes to rest
on the edge of the bath, level with my eyes.
She's a Large White – I'd been praying
to see one soon – and her wings quiver
in the steamy heat of the water.
She flits to my stomach, settles between
my thighs. Then others fly in:
Red Admirals, Painted Ladies, more Large Whites,
a mass of wings fanning the glow
in a swirl of colour, till their flutter
giddies me in a breathless rainbow rush
and they're flying off to another fourteen year old boy.
It was better than scoring a penalty,
even mother sending money.
I tell myself I'll give up the butterflies
when I've seen them ten times,
but after I get to double figures, I lose count.

Bathtime Butterflies at Boarding School appeared in Wide Skies, Salt and Best Bitter, published by Hearing Eye, 2005. © Peter

Phillips. Reprinted by permission of Hearing Eye.

PART II – MAKING SENSE OF IT ALL

(Ages 40-56)

Leo

The Child is Father of the Man

As far as I am concerned I just feel like me and I can't really describe it in any way which is going to be meaningful to anyone else. I can only say what my reaction is to particular situations. This might give other people some indication of what it is like to be me. I feel sad or happy; these might just be words which mean different things to me and to other people. How do other people know what I really feel like if I feel happy or sad? The chemical reactions working within my brain might be the same as other people's but can I be sure that the sensation they feel is exactly or approximately the same?

I feel happier with pictures than with words. I remember going to the National Gallery as a young child and the colours, the smell and the whole aura of the world of pictures fascinated me. The images remain in my memory and since then a particular kind of red or a rich dark blue has always evoked vivid memories leading me on to recall particular scenes and stories. The power of pictures has always been more powerful than the power of words. Much of my thinking appears to be in pictorial images rather than in words. I always wonder what it is like for other people; do other people always think in words or for them is it in pictures? And if so, do they see the same pictures as me?

I remember especially landscape pictures of the kind painted by Claude Lorraine. My father used to tell me a story of a man who used to go into art galleries, sit himself in front of a picture and after a while would nod off and dream that he was part of what was being depicted. I felt the same. I used what was before me on the gallery wall to build up an imaginary world all of my own, then fill it up with my own figures, stories and emotions. But what did other people feel when they looked at the same painting? Were they experiencing the same feelings? Did they see the same things as I did and could we, through some extraordinary act of the will, join hands and step through the frame into another world and see and experience exactly the same things, a bit like the children stepping through the wardrobe into Narnia?

So how did the person next to me react to the same picture? Or was what I was seeing something completely and particularly everything to do with me? We probably saw the same physical things; a tree here or a lake there, a group of wood nymphs to the left and shepherds to the right, but did they really mean the same thing to him or her as they did to me? Not only in terms of what they were but also in the sense of what meaning they give to their life? Probably not, because each element of the picture has for me its own associations. A particular wood or tree might bring to mind a tree I saw on a walk or a holiday some time ago; the nymphs and shepherds with stories learnt at my mother's knee; the overall picture with conversations with friends over a number of years. I can even associate pictures with particular moods but again this is a mood which is the product of my own personal history and experience.

However, this uncertainty about what people are seeing also means I am unsure about what other people are feeling and about how I interact with others, especially since most of the time I feel as though I have no identity. Other people appear to have such rich emotional and thinking lives. I can't say that I am always aware of how I feel. Walking along the street often I completely lose my identity; I do not think and I just react to what I see in the shop windows or on the road. Don't expect anything meaningful there; just an ordinary human brain functioning on autopilot.

I do have some difficulty with communication and trying to make sense of what is happening around me, especially when somebody tries to break into my inner world, the world of nymphs and fairies where it is always early evening. At work or during the normal course of everyday contact people start talking to me. My immediate reaction is one of panic and confusion and breaking out in a cold sweat. What are they going to say to me and will I understand what they are saying? Their first few sentences always confuse me. I desperately try to find in their words something which I can identify or hold on to; a word or a phrase that means something to me. Once I've spotted that familiar word or phrase my mind tries to grasp what is being said; it goes through all the various lines of association to pick up what the other person might be talking about. Usually at a certain point I pick up the right meaning embedded somewhere in my memory and everything starts to fall into place. It's much easier if somebody is asking me for factual information which I either know or don't know.

Having picked up the right message I feel much closer to the person who has spoken to me. I immediately feel that here is a fellow human being, someone with whom I can share at least part of my experiences as a fellow human being. Perhaps this to me is my purest and simplest form of communicating with people. But what if it is still unclear what the other person is talking about? My sense of confusion and unease increases; there is no point of contact. Perhaps they are talking at a different intellectual level? Does this make them much more intelligent than me or does it mean that there are people around who live in a totally different world from me?

However, I don't live in a complete vacuum and although I might spend much of my life thinking about nothing or living in fear that people will catch me unawares, at least it doesn't happen all the time. I can strike up friendships. These friendships force me to look at and outside myself. This can itself be rather discomforting. I find I can be easily influenced by people around me. I am forced to think when I'm in the presence of or talking to other people, and I'm not used to that. Sometimes it is easier to remain silent; allow people to talk whilst holding back oneself. I really don't want to let on that I have no view on a subject or that I don't really understand what the other person is talking about.

Other people apparently find it easy to strike up conversations or dialogue on the basis of firmly held opinions or beliefs. I find it rather difficult myself. I read omnivorously but find it difficult to retain what I've read; I mean to remember the interesting fact or the key quotation which sums up the meaning of life, but somehow it slips my memory. Perhaps, like the Victorians, I should compile an 'everyday' book full of snippets of what I've read but unfortunately I've never got round to it. Consequently, I find the words and ideas are still jumbled in my head. I am, therefore, constantly taken by surprise. I can start off a conversation but then I'm not sure how to continue it. Either the person with whom I'm talking knows more about the subject than I do and so I become disheartened, or else they don't appear interested, in which case I also become disheartened.

I remember a friend who had read a lot, thought a lot and formulated opinions on most topics under the sun, such as the role of the medieval concept of usury in the rise of capitalism. I'd read a few books on the subject but since reading these books hadn't really thought about the issue and certainly hadn't come to an overall view on the subject. I'd only read enough to write a serviceable answer to an exam question or to feel happy that I had a reasonable knowledge of the existence of a possible problem. I'd never tried to incorporate it into my overall worldview of history.

Therefore, when I am forced to consider any subject on which I should rightly have some opinion, I find that my mind goes blank or else I remember that I did read something about it but cannot remember where or what. The result is that I am often forced to agree with whatever is said to me. This makes me appear to my interlocutor as a very amenable person who has a similar opinion to him or her on most subjects. Similarly, in the field of emotions; people who are more forthcoming on how they feel will probably find in me a sympathetic listener but not someone who will come out up front with his own emotions. I do feel that I am often an intellectual or emotional chameleon changing my colour or character according to the person with whom I'm talking.

Perhaps this is a matter of confidence or lack of confidence in my own values or intellectual ability. I believe I may have had such confidence in certain values or beliefs when I was growing up but that was just the result of a secure and comfortable childhood. All the values I held seemed so self evident and there was no reason to question them. Everyone I know seemed to be happy and secure in living out what appeared to be permanent and objective values within a well-ordered lifestyle. This is one of the advantages of living in a closely-knit family in a similarly closely-knit faith and ethnic community where everyone did or strived to do what was self evidently right. Perhaps this has influenced my rather conformist attitude to this day. Although I can see many reasons why one can and does question so many things, be they beliefs or behaviours, I could never see any reason to disrupt or not act in accordance with such beliefs or behaviours where they produced the apparently right result. Why not continue to believe in the traditional Christian God when such beliefs resulted in altruistic behaviour as well as fine music and art? I could accept most of the Ten Commandments because really the behaviour they prohibited didn't seem to be particularly tempting, and even if it did there appeared to be any number of escape clauses. Life seemed to be so much more enjoyable when I had my behaviour planned out for me. I thought I knew what I could expect of other people. It also allowed me to channel my acts of rebellion in a very ordered way. I liked to know that somebody had set certain limits to what I could do and I felt no reason to go any further.

However, it's always come as a bit of a shock to me to realise that not everyone close to me might share what to me are quite fundamental values. Perhaps the most striking example of this is promiscuity, not just physical promiscuity but, more importantly perhaps, emotional promiscuity. I grew up believing that it is very important for one to be completely open and faithful to one's true friends. When I went to university I was quite shocked to find that, at a very basic level, personal relationships could be reduced to something very superficial and random. Friendships could be made and broken due to the circumstances of the moment. To me relationships had to be built up and had always to be open to development. Even the briefest encounter should have within it the possibility of a closer and more intimate knowledge of what the other person is. Perhaps this has made me somewhat idealistic in my attitude to relationships and knowing what high standards I set I have tended to shy away from possible friendships. Knowing how much I expect of a relationship or friendship and knowing that I need to invest so much time and effort in building and maintaining the friendship, I have tended to be a little reserved in putting myself forward. Perhaps it's a fear that I will be sucked dry or, having given myself completely to it, I'll be rejected. In the end the friend will not think me worth the effort.

This is why, although not naturally an active person, I have tended to be a joiner of organisations. It's not sufficient that I just talk about issues; people are not going to admire me just because of that. I have to be seen to do something. People will then have to take notice. I might not come up with the inspirational moments of leadership or provide magnificent insights into people's souls, but I can organise agendas, chair meetings, write letters and stack up the furniture at the end of events. That, at least, gives me some right to have a view on things and gives me some claim, if not to people's friendship, at least to their good opinion. Something along the lines of people's opinion of Captain Wentworth in *Persuasion*; that although many people might respect me, nobody can love me. This perhaps has always been a part of my character, that I have to earn people's love. It will not come free.

Do I consciously try to model myself on others or go out of my way to please? I do tend to seek people's good opinion. One of the few occasions I felt uncomfortable at school was when I was told that I was an unreliable person, since then I have tried to make a point of being the person on whom people can rely; trying, sometimes unsuccessfully, to be the person in the audience or congregation who can be called upon in any emergency. It is a case of setting high, sometimes impossible, standards for myself. I like being asked to do things or being asked for help. Perhaps this does mean that I lack self-confidence. Perhaps I am trying to find ways to show myself what I am worth by setting myself challenges or hurdles or having other people set targets for me. At school and at university I liked to be told what was expected of me. I found it difficult to set my own standards and targets. This instilled in me a propensity to defer to the will or advice of others. They set me the target which I accepted as my own, since then I've always welcomed imposed and later self-imposed targets. Perhaps again this is an awareness that without these targets my inclination would be to do nothing. It is satisfying to know that having completed these tasks or hit my targets I will have proved to myself and others that there is something else I know or can do. However, what I'm not sure about is whether, if others were not about to approve or applaud my actions, I would do anything at all. Is my own feeling of self-approval sufficient to keep me going? If nobody other than I existed in the world would this sense of self-achievement wither away? If there is no one around to see what I'm doing should I still try?

Central to most of the things I do is a sense of duty. I find it rare that I do something out of a pure act of love or enthusiasm. I feel as though I lack spontaneity. What other people say they do out of love I find I do out of duty. I take nothing for granted when I meet or visit someone, a relative or a friend. From what I can see it requires a supreme act of relaxation for me to be totally comfortable. But then again, I need to know beforehand what I can talk about in order to build up the rapport. Otherwise, I can't see how my company is going to add to their pleasure. So I do find I do things often out of a sense of duty. This is not to say that I do not enjoy myself when and after meeting the other person but the initial moments often bring with them a possible feeling of foreboding, some disaster in the making. Sometimes I feel I am going through the motions, as though I were an emotional automaton. However, at a certain stage, this sense of doing things from a sense of duty does translate into something warmer. Shared experiences, feelings, jokes and glances lead on to the warmth of human affection and love.

Some people have particularly vivid dreams which stay with them during their waking hours. I know I dream but as soon as I wake up the images of my dream fall away almost completely. I sometimes think I'm missing out. How come other people have dreams that stay with them? For me, sleep is a complete blank. My last minutes of thoughts at night before I fall asleep continue in the morning. My first thoughts in the morning are usually: where was I and what was I worrying about last thing at night? Although I enjoy my sleep I sometimes think it is time wasted. For other people, sleep and the dreams they have during their sleep might enrich their emotional life; for me, it's almost a complete blank. However, I have to say 'almost', because every now and again I am aware of recurrent images and dreams. In fact, these fall into mainly two categories. Firstly, the examinations for which I have forgotten to do any preparation or study; I've just started my third and final year at university and I can't remember what subject I'm reading. Secondly, I'm continuing to live in my family home even though I have long since sold it and expect the new owners to move in at any time, although they never do.

Perhaps as one gets older one gets grumpier but I find it increasingly difficult to get excited by the prospect of exotic holidays, more money or more high-powered cars. This sometimes worries me. But I occasionally think of the funeral address by a priest who, talking of a family friend, said he seemed to laugh at life and what other people thought to be of importance. He seemed to be completely uninterested. Perhaps I feel the same. When it comes down to it I think, 'What am I other than a construction of billions of cells, which could very well have been brought to life in some other form – part of an amoeba, for example?' It's sufficient that this collection of cells should be able to enjoy even momentarily the exhilaration of walking along Beachy Head in a force-ten gale, oblivious to what went before and what comes after. My happiest moments are when I can completely enjoy the sensations of the moment without having to think of what I have done to get there or what lies in store in the future, even in the next moment. My collection of cells celebrates what they are, there and then. What does the prospect of more money mean in such moments of pure happiness? Not a lot. The real prospect of an after-life is the complete enjoyment of being on a park swing, going higher and higher, no past or future, just one complete and eternal moment of happiness.

Mark

A Bit about Mark

I believe that what it feels like to be me is as a result of both my personality traits and my experiences in life, i.e. both nature and nurture. Therefore, I have tried to cover both of these attributes to give you a good idea of what it feels like to be me.

My memories of childhood are generally positive. My father enjoyed canoeing (kayaking) and we went camping most weekends so that Dad could canoe. My sister, Sarah (who is 17 months older than me) and I loved camping in the typical New Zealand facilities in the 1970s of 'bare minimum' – not in a camping ground, but in a National Park or a farmers paddock where there were no facilities or running water. My mother didn't canoe but spent her weekends looking after us around the campsite while Dad canoed. She would cover herself in baby-oil and bake in the sun. Back then there were not the concerns about skin cancer and the other consequences of too much sun. The weekends spent camping were enjoyable and relaxing. Sarah and I had some great adventures, and we both still enjoy camping and the outdoors (although now that I am older I prefer a bit more luxury than sleeping on the hard ground).

I remember camping one Easter at a place where Dad canoed; Mum and Dad hid our Easter eggs in the paddock that we were camping in. We had to find them before the cows stood on them. Sarah and I remember that holiday and having to find the eggs, and it's those sorts of enjoyable experiences that I want my children to remember.

As well as camping most weekends, for our long summer vacation we would go camping at the beautiful white sandy beaches up north. Sarah and I would spend the hot, sunny days swimming and exploring the rock pools. We'd make friends with other kids at the camp ground, but we'd also be happy just playing together. We used to leave home at midnight to drive north and arrive at the camping ground just as dawn was breaking. It was always exciting getting ready to go away. We would have a shower and then get carried to Mum and Dad's chairs in the lounge (so that we didn't get dirty again) and we would have to stay in those chairs until we were carried out to the car. The reason Mum and Dad were so particular about us staying clean was that in the car we sat on top of all the bedding needed for the holiday. The rear seats were piled up to the level of the windows. The ironic thing was that as soon as we stopped for petrol Sarah and I would leap out of the car and run across the dirty forecourt to go to the toilet, then get back onto the bedding – so much for keeping it clean.

When I was about nine years old Mum and Dad bought a 20 foot sailboat that we could sleep aboard – so our camping holidays ended and we went sailing most weekends instead. That brought different adventures. Sarah and I would row ashore and explore the foreshore, or swim off the boat.

My sister and I got on really well, with very little arguing or fighting, although now I reflect on my childhood, I think our good relationship was largely due to me being so placid and accommodating with whatever she wanted to do or play. I see a lot of similarities of my personality in my son, Jared (currently ten years old), who, like me, likes to please people and dislikes confrontation. He often goes out of his way to help his older sister, Nicole, who is 12, and his younger sister, Jessica, who is seven. And like my sister in our relationship, Nicole seems to dominate her siblings, influencing what they will play. Jared's always ready for school first and will often go upstairs and make his sisters' beds so that they'll be ready in time for school. He's always the first to offer to share and go without when there's an argument over something like the last biscuit or a toy.

I certainly have no regrets about not standing up to my sister, and going along generally with her wishes, as that is my personality and to do anything different would not have felt comfortable. It's not that we didn't have disagreements, but they're not what I immediately remember, as it's the positive times that I instantly recall. On reflection, I remember one fight we had where Sarah pushed my face into the couch, and as I had braces at the time, my braces got caught on the couch and I was stuck. It's funny now, but it wasn't at the time.

Sarah and I spent ages pushing each other around on home built go-karts – up and down the street. Back in the 1970s there wasn't the same concern about strangers and before we were even teenagers we were able, along with some friends from up the road, to go on what we called 'mystery walks'. It was always a mystery where we would end up. We would wander around the streets and across farmland. The rule was that we had to be home when the 'street lights came on' or when we got hungry – whichever came first. Thinking about it now, our parents had no idea where we were and what we were doing. Not that we got up to mischief, but I wouldn't give my kids the same freedom, mainly because I'm concerned with their safety.

My paternal grandparents also had a strong influence on my childhood development. My grandparents would always drop what they were doing and give us their undivided attention. They frequented garage sales and used to buy and sell things. It was always fun going to their place and seeing what new things they had purchased. My grandfather also had a model railway in his garage and when I was older I would cycle across town and spend the day helping him make houses and roads for the railway. I wasn't interested in the trains, but more interested in the landscaping, houses, etc. I remember sometimes putting little things across the tracks and causing derailments. He would spend ages sanding the track trying to work out why the train had derailed. I guess he knew I had caused it, but he just humoured me. He also taught me how to drive. He was very patient. Every Saturday morning we would drive around the garage sales. It was a great way to learn to drive, and there was the thrill of not knowing what would be at the next garage sale. Back then garage sales had not become popular as a way to find bargains, so it was amazing what could be bought for just a few dollars.

When I was 11, our childhood was turned upside down when our mother decided that she wanted to separate from our father. Being immature and not knowing much about separation I initially thought that the change would be exciting, but that soon changed when I released the full consequences. My mother had, up to that point, done everything around the house, perhaps contributing to her decision to move out, not that she would have permitted anyone else to take more responsibility as we would not have done the jobs to her very high standard. When she moved out she promised Dad that because she had initiated the separation she wouldn't take Sarah and me with her. This decision was probably also motivated by the fact that the man that she had moved out to be with was eight years her junior and didn't have children. So when Mum moved out Dad, Sarah and I struggled with learning how to do the usual household jobs – cooking, washing and ironing. Together we managed, and I guess later in life it helped when I went flatting. Initially mum wasn't too far away and we were able to see her quite frequently, but after a while she and her new partner moved to a city several hours away. As Sarah and I were too young to drive, we relied on the coach service to visit during school holidays. Dad was really good and wanted to encourage our relationship with Mum so when we learnt to drive he lent us his car so that we could visit her.

Although Mum and I had a closer relationship than Mum and Sarah, the divorce probably affected Sarah more than me. No one knows how events like this change people's personality. The reason I say that Sarah was probably affected more than me was because Sarah was reaching the age of being interested in boys and would have benefited from the advice, and perhaps control, from a mother that was closer and more involved. Mum was never a warm affectionate person. She didn't, and still doesn't, like hugs and cuddles. It's not that she doesn't love us; it's just that she is not very tactile. Even now when my kids rush up to her to give her a big hug she pushes them away with some excuse or another. Mum shows her affection differently – through doing things for people. I don't hold any resentment against Mum's decision to move out – she had to do what she felt was right at the time.

Anyway, less of others and more about myself:

Perhaps the events during my childhood have caused me to have my strong sense of responsibility. I wouldn't cause the same disruption to my children, not that I would consider separating from my wife as we're happily married. Sure, like any relationship there are definitely ups and downs but fortunately my wife, Annette, doesn't sulk or get moody for too long and we work through our issues – not that I remember my parents arguing very frequently.

I try to ensure that my kids have every possibility in life and I hope that they have an enjoyable childhood and look back on it with fond memories. One reason we have come to England is to expose the kids to different cultures and experiences. Being honest though, it's not totally an unselfish move, because both Annette and I always wanted to live and work in England. Whether the kids appreciate this experience we'll only know later in their lives. In some way I hope this experience will also get the travelling bug out of their systems so that when they're older, they won't venture too far from home. Selfish I know, but I think it would be great if they wanted to live close to Annette and me.

I was a loner at school. I am happy and content with my own company, without the need to be surrounded by others. I get drained when I'm with a large group and rejuvenate when I have time to myself. I always remember when I was at primary school being told by another boy that he was going to be a loner, but his dad suggested it wasn't a good idea. He made the statement as though he had a choice in the matter rather than it being a personality trait. Even at work I'm introverted, and prefer not to make contributions in joint discussions. I always think it's better to keep quiet and be thought of as an idiot rather than to open my mouth and prove that I'm an idiot.

I believe that my life is what I make of it and it's important to have a positive outlook on life. I'm a strong believer in the concept of the glass being half full rather than half empty. I always take time out during a day to enjoy the wonderful world we live in, whether that be the crisp clear morning, listening to a particular piece of music that is special, or looking at the amazing vapour trails left by aeroplanes that criss-cross the sky. These vapour trails look even more amazing when there's a red sunset. We certainly don't get as many vapour trails in New Zealand – there aren't nearly as many planes! I always remember camping in a little tent in the middle of nowhere in New Zealand and a Boeing 747 passing overhead. I thought at the time about the contrast: I was removed from civilisation with no running water and sleeping on the ground, while immediately overhead were several hundred people heading off to somewhere exotic and exciting. Taking time to look at the wonderful things in life – which are often very simple things – helps reduce the possible humdrum of everyday existence.

I try and get my kids to experience new things in life; some things they may not enjoy and never want to do again and others may cause total exhilaration. A few years ago we started 'taste nights'. I was concerned that the kids were not keen to try new and different foods. They were often 'put off' trying something simply by how it looked or what it was called, rather than from actually trying it; so once a week we'd try a food that we hadn't had before. Annette doesn't like seafood so the kids had not experienced scallops, crayfish, oysters, etc, so we got the kids to try a new food each week. Most of the time it went well, but sometimes the appearance of the food made it a bit of a battle to get them to eat it. I must admit that mussels do not appear that appetising especially when certain parts have to be removed before they can be eaten, and when I explained that a small dark area was the 'pooh' sack, well, there was no way they were going to eat it then!

As there are three kids (that are often quite competitive for Annette's and my attention), I try to take a child out of the family situation and sit down and listen to his or her concerns. I try and find out if they have any issues and hopefully provide them with some tools and alternatives to deal with those problems. They enjoy the time without their siblings and not having to compete for our attention. Hopefully they take on board my suggestions, but as they get older I think that more of my suggestions will be dismissed in preference to the advice from their peer groups. I just have to accept that.

I believe that I am very fortunate – with having a wonderful loving wife and three healthy and generally happy kids, and hopefully I can provide them with some great experiences that they'll remember and put them in a good position for their adult life.

Dominic

Always Searching for 'Self'

'Always searching for 'self'.' What does this mean? That we do not like the selves that we are? Or we are not comfortable with our ability to project our selves, our personality on others? Or we are too aware of our desire to conform, to fit in?

We have different expressions of self: the self that wants to be recognised in our most intimate relationships; the self we project in social and occupational situations; the self that is reflected in what we do; a self that reflects the values we hold, or, indeed, the community or place we come from; self as a member of a family; and the self that results from our sexuality – identity as man or woman.

So far 'self' does not seem very individual, rooted as it seems to be in family, community or landscape. It seems a paradox that the self thrives when it benefits from these factors and suffers when left alone.

For most of my life I have felt like a chameleon, responding to the demands of the different situations I have moved into. Responding, not absorbing, not processing. I have been aware of a self that I have wanted to be, but have felt too unconfident to listen to that inner voice. I had no sense of self to adequately manage different situations and challenges. Instead, I tried to respond to their demands. Boarding school, in particular, required a strategy for survival and roles to survive.

Childhood was played out in four locations: colonial Africa where I was born, boarding school, Ireland and England. It had some dislocating factors: the boarding school was in a foreign country among an alien class and culture; there was prolonged separation from parents and immediate family; it required moving between the ethos of a public school and an Irish working class setting. The common factor was a Catholic experience and identity which took deep root in otherwise barren soil.

Africa

I never felt totally at home in Africa. The European presence did not have the feel of permanence. There was an exotic quality but we seemed to have no real stake in the country or continent. I – and I think the family – did not find a way to properly engage with the country or with its people. As a very young child I often wondered what life would be like in England, where we would live, and what type of house we would have. There was uncertainty. That is not to say the African experience had no meaning. I was, after all, born there; I later went back to work there; I represented one of the regions at sport; and I read for a postgraduate degree on the area. However, while it tugs at my conscience I can make no connection that speaks to identity.

Ireland

A positive aspect in those early years was holidays spent in Ireland with the extended family. The community I experienced seemed to generate a level of acceptance of individuals and their behaviour.

It was, I later learned, a 'face to face' society. People's social interactions mattered but within that there seemed to be a degree of acceptance of individuals and their idiosyncrasies. Even the half crazed old woman who lived up the street and whose antics were driven by drink seemed to contribute to the interest of daily life. If there was a degree of criticism it was offset by acknowledgement of the contribution she made – at the very least she allowed others to feel superior. It seemed that the community had embraced diversity. Social acceptance was also underpinned by economic reality: in a world of small shopkeepers and tradesmen and of limited money you tolerate others because they are your customers.

It was pre-television Ireland and most of the culture was social. People were literate rather than literary. The psychological frame of reference was more outdoors than in: it seemed to matter more what impact one made within the community than within one's own family. Truth was what was said to be so; people reported their conversations and the audience could align their views to respect the status of the speaker.

All of this social interaction was played out against a background of basic survival. There was a relative cultural poverty which was a reflection of relative real poverty; both of which had implications for family and personal relationships. I was later to contrast the experience of my wife's Welsh grandmother and mine. My grandmother's pride as a cook was not, like my wife's, reflected in her own alternative version of *Mrs Beeton's Cookbook* but in the frequency with which she had been able to put meat on the table. I remember being enjoined by mine to eat one slice of bread for each sausage or rasher: one should not take the provision of meat for granted.

In that community the primary parental role seemed to be the provision of shelter, food and clothing. Much of the educational role was provided by the extended family, the school and the Church (priests or nuns). It was not unusual for a child in a medium-to-large sized family to live with a relative who had more space. In my own family I can think of examples in each of three successive generations of relatives.

The generational relationships were or could be marked by inequalities which were a reflection of power. Those inequalities would be addressed by time: the younger generation would later have their turn to be dominant. Mothers tended to favour sons, no doubt looking forward to the realities of widowed old age. Children could and were expected to entertain but usually their views did not count: as they were not economic players they did not have to be listened to. There seemed little social mobility; those who wanted movement, left. Those who stayed seemed to sign up for immobility and mutual acceptance. A negative aspect of this social acceptance was, I later came to think, that individuals could grow up psychologically unchallenged: too unquestioned and unquestioning.

There seemed to be a number of 'givens' in this community and even those who left were probably heavily conditioned by them. This was the world my parents grew up in and for a short while I benefited from some of the same factors that had shaped them: I benefited from the preferential treatments of boys; one of my sisters suffered the opposite. But it was the degree of acceptance that registered most. Ireland to me was an oasis in a childhood that otherwise proved to be an emotional desert, but those holidays came to an end too early. I look on them as a time when I enjoyed the unconditional warmth of the wider family. I took the benefit without understanding the context. The critique above is the result of subsequent attempts to understand the psychological differences that separated me and my parents.

Although they left Ireland in their mid-twenties my parents remained psychologically conditioned by their upbringing. They had a deeper sense of parental duty than basic provision but they unconsciously carried with them the sense that the wider family and community provided some of the emotional support. Their experience did not prepare them for the needs of a child uprooted too early. They had little consciousness of such a state or any sense that their sacrifice in providing education could be perceived as an act of separation and rejection. Their inability to understand left me perplexed and reinforced the sense of rejection. Awareness of their sacrifice prevented me communicating the experience of school.

They also processed their experiences in their own way. My mother came from a large family and resented the preferential treatment given to her brothers, a pattern she was determined would not be repeated in her family.

School

The environment I grew up in was heavily religious. My parents were devout and membership of the church was a major part of their identity. As a young person I took religion very seriously. I internalised at quite a deep level many of the values and tried to conduct myself as expected. At school and in Ireland I went to confession and communion frequently, mass almost daily.

I never felt that I belonged at school. I did not come from the right social background, notwithstanding the social step up that the overseas experience tended to give. There was a disconnection between term time and holidays, at times a painful difference. Religion bridged the gap. The school, run by monks, had free places for would-be priests from less privileged backgrounds. Though my parents paid the fees I felt more identity with those boys and more secure in expressing a religious identity. There developed an expectation that I would join the monastery.

Religion can be very damaging to the self. The Christian message can be interpreted as requiring the total denial of self. I contrast the form of religious upbringing and education which I experienced with that of therapy – also as experienced. The former, particularly through the confessional, tends to concentrate on the negative aspects of personality and behaviour, the latter on trying to arrive at a positive assessment, warts and all. In recent years I have heard more positive messages from Catholic priests, closer to those of the therapist. I still find it strange to hear a priest say that it is necessary to love one – that was not the message I heard in earlier years.

The tradition of Catholicism can present particular difficulties in relation to sexuality. It can come over as a near complete denial and the message was usually given by people who had signed up to that denial. What might be considered normal thought processes and fantasies of adolescence are 'impure thoughts' and, of course sin. There can be a problem with absorbing such a message at too early an age. Any sin can be seen as failure of character – an equation that the priests were very good at making. For me the onset of adolescence was quite devastating. Not only did the aspiration for the priesthood and perfection disappear but the concept of self as worthy of respect and focus could not stand up to scrutiny. Not only had the idealised self disappeared but at the core it was so lacking in moral fibre it was not capable of being a base for anything. Focus on priesthood had been much more than a temporary construct of convenience designed to let me manage my situation. The aspiration had been deeply internalised and the loss was that much greater.

There was an outer life to school – the life that one had to live through to survive. Many people now will not understand the ethos of such schools at a time when we still had an empire. Implicitly or explicitly people were developed for roles in such a world. The educational system was designed to change you. This required breaking you down with well known rituals – fagging, bullying, strict discipline, corporal punishment, etc – and rebuilding. Fifth form bullying of fourth formers (new boys) was treated as a rite of passage for both. The experience was to a degree brutalising. But rebuilding was necessary. I thought the school did not know how to rebuild, institutionally too insecure to make a choice between the monastic ideal and the standard ethos of such schools. To the extent that it veered towards the latter, in my view it made the wrong choice. And I wondered how the monks could preside over the institution they were responsible for. The philosophy of the school was 'sink or swim'. I doggy paddled. At a basic level I survived. There was a muscular sporting side which was fairly dominant and I was good at one sport. It was a point of connection, a lifeline. Without it I might have sunk. To others that was my identify as well as my passport to acceptance – a response that I came to resent. Externally, it was probably a stronger identity than that of the would-be priest.

The paradox of that boarding school, which was imbued to some degree with monastic ideals and discipline, was that the 'aloneness' gave time to develop an inner life but the fact that one was not sharing that inner world left one unconfident about what was being developed. There was no external validation, no one to suggest that the inner world had value, to encourage you to find yourself, find out what you might want to do or become. Nor was there any mirroring at home. The external reality of school was daily survival and accommodation, learning how to fulfil some role or other in society. But there was a major disconnection between what I felt and how I behaved. Both school and home and my inner and outer worlds seemed endlessly compartmentalised and unrelated.

I can remember the time of greatest unhappiness at school being alone on the rugby pitches kicking a ball around and thinking that there was no one I could turn to. The sense of depth of that aloneness is a feeling that I have never fully shaken; that time on those pitches a moment to which I have sometimes returned. One of the ways I have carried this forward is to feel that I need always to be prepared to lose everything that I have; and I have to rely on myself in all situations. It has been very hard to see one of my children replicate some of that sense of isolation and enforced self reliance.

With hindsight, I can see that the experience on those fields contained within it the kernel of the development of a survivor but the quality of that survival is questionable. The sense of the ability to survive that I took away from the day to day accommodations was basic and primitive. It contributed nothing to my emotional, social or intellectual development. I am conscious that the legacy of that time is still with me and when apparent is unattractive.

England

After three years at boarding school, Africa became England

when the nation in which my parents worked achieved independence. I was now to spend three holidays with them and my sisters instead of one. Geographical proximity did not bring us closer emotionally. They were concentrating on establishing themselves in a new country – for one it involved a completely new career – and had no sense of a need to catch up with children they had not seen much of in recent years.

There were emerging differences between us in attitude and understanding founded on different social and cultural experiences: theirs still significantly informed by the Ireland of their youth; mine affected by the experiences of the recent years to which there appeared no end. Unlike them, I felt severely psychologically challenged. There was not any aspect of myself that I did not question. Over a prolonged period I was even to question my ability to read and think. I was not the compliant dutiful son they expected. My enforced independent behaviour clashed with their perception of how a child fitted in. I wanted recognition for the loss of our primary relationship. The gap between us was not obviously bridged by affection. Their lack of understanding and my inability to kindle affection in them confirmed me in my isolation.

My father's view of parenthood was primarily biological which then found expression in social norms and expectations. For both there was a 'matter of fact' approach to parenthood, raised to a higher level by duty but detained from development by day to day concerns. My father seemed unable to cope either with my failures or any successes as he struggled with his new career. While he was to spend the rest of his life helping disadvantaged boys it came as no surprise that he never came to terms with the therapeutic side of the work.

Their marriage was not a love match: it was love on her side, obligation on his. It was not always happy or in equilibrium. Theirs was the dominant relationship and it consumed the emotional resources of the family. As a small child I had put together facts of their coming together from pieces of information that were leaked in frustration. It caused me considerable distress, and to doubt why I had come into existence. At times I felt an obstacle to their separation and their hopes for a more contented life. The period starting with their settling into England was also not the easiest of times in their marriage, and difficult though school was I preferred its austere and emotionally sterile stability. Looking back I take some limited pride in surviving. I might have found the overall experience of those years overwhelming but having alternative bases of operations (home and school) allowed for some psychological arbitrage which helped me to manage the situation.

Leaving School

I did not join the monastery. In truth it had ceased to be a serious option about two years before I left the school. I knew that I was emotionally and intellectually unprepared. I no longer thought I had a vocation; I also think I subconsciously understood the need for an intimate relationship in which I would find some degree of acceptance.

Those last two years were a very difficult time. I felt I was going backwards, if not disintegrating. I could see my peers growing in confidence. I could see no connection between my compartmentalised worlds and the world I was going to have to operate in. I believe I experienced some form of nervous breakdown although it was neither diagnosed nor acknowledged at the time and would not have been distinguished by those around me from the behaviour of an inadequate adolescent. I failed to get into university.

I was totally unprepared for the real world. I could not relate and struggled to cope. I had learned to survive in an institution but I emerged emotionally and socially very underdeveloped. There had been few and limited friendships, usually ending in some form of failure. I felt insulated from girls by my sheer unattractiveness, that isolation further sealed by the emotional preparation for priesthood. I was to struggle in the mixed educational environment that followed school when young women called me by my first name: I was only used to being called by my surname or a variant on it.

The following ten years were spent trying to achieve some level of normality. In that time I was to benefit from a few valuable friendships and from operating in a friendlier environment. Eventually I went to university and emerged from it with some confidence. I married and have three children. However, the unprocessed past has been a heavy legacy.

Legacy

The pattern that had been set by the time I left school was one of intense inner isolation. Also I was conscious of the contrast between my inner self and the self-projected on the world in order to survive. This dichotomy passed into adult life. I have also been aware of and driven by two tensions, both of which reflect earlier experiences: an awareness of the opportunities that my parents' sacrifice seemed to give me but which I have never fully been able to take advantage of, and a desire to establish and be confident in what I wanted to do.

A major cost has been the enclosure in a private world and to some degree in the past. It has not been possible to discuss the past – mostly because people are not interested or are not able to relate to the experiences one would like to communicate. I feel like a veteran from a war that few have heard of and fewer are interested in and yet the experience explains in part who he is and where he is now. That 'war' is now hardly a footnote in a social history. But those experiences do not go away because they have engendered issues that need to be addressed. Even siblings who, *prima facie*, have been through parallel experiences, never seem to have shown much or, indeed, any comprehension. The lack of response or willingness of others to engage has made me doubt my experiences and their value.

I have, I believe, a developed sense of self as a survivor. But it is limited: it is borne from a sense of a need to survive rather than any pride in doing so. School not only provided the first major requirement to do so but also conveyed a subliminal message that life is about survival. One carries on the same behaviour but in a wider context.

I do not equate isolation with complete self sufficiency. I am grateful for kindness, recognition, empathy. But I am also afraid of what would happen if the inner walls were to be completely undermined by that kindness, etc.

Relationships

I have struggled with relationships, in part because of the ingrained sense of isolation and its causes. I have sometimes wondered whether I have a degree of autism, not as a result of physiological dysfunction but social conditioning, a process that may have started when as a very young child I was sent to a sanatorium with scarlet fever and, because isolated, refused to speak. At times my wife has found trying to deal with the legacy of the past to be too much.

Unfinished?

My inability to process has left me somewhat paralysed. I have performed in certain areas but I have not felt that I have fully engaged. I think my performance would have been better had I been able to fully align myself with what I do. I have tended to operate in situations which require technical ability. Where leadership has been required I have been able to perform provided there has been a structure to recognise authority or I have relied on the authority of technical input. I feel that I have some interpersonal skills but hesitate to rely on them.

Maslow's *Hierarchy of Needs* suggests a useful basis of categorisation – with modification – of the different selves and identities we may espouse. At a very basic level, there is a self which needs to know that it can survive economically and (in a minimal sense) socially in the world. Beyond that there is a self that will flourish in the most intimate relationships; then the self we project in social and occupational situations; then the self that is reflected in what we do and what we achieve; and finally a self that is projected in the values we hold. My points of identification along this scale are a sense that I am largely stuck at the economic and minimally social stage and to the extent that I get beyond that I seek and take value in achievement, as a basis of recognition and identity.

Sexuality is one of our identities. I grew up with at least three role models: a version of Irish manhood, the officer/administrator of empire and the monk. I can see all three reflected in me but not as a fully reconciled outcome or synthesis or as a choice made for one.

But even if experiences are unprocessed they are still there. The fact that they appear as tensions does not negate their importance to you. At the end of the day there always is a self even if we are uncomfortable with the result or feel too tentative to show it.

Religion

There is considerable overlap in the spheres of religion and psychotherapy. I find myself sometimes talking to the therapist in the way that I would like to talk to a priest. I have developed a considerable aversion to confession as it is ordinarily experienced. I have wondered whether the roll out of institution of confessor beyond narrow elite might provide an experience closer to that of therapy.

A little while ago I found myself trying to make a decision between entering therapy and trying to work out my inner concerns in a conventional religious context – prayer, greater commitment. I saw it in part as the old dilemma of submission of self (religious route) and a degree of indulgence (therapy). I thought the time had come to make a conscious effort to further discipline my emotions and to try to find some contentment in late middle age. I chose to try the former but I was to reverse that decision.

Finding a Process?

A great deal from my past has stayed with me. I have not wanted to reject it all. I identify with many of the values of my background: monastic school and home. What has been missing is a strong enough self that is capable of processing those values and experiences and fully making them my own. There is nothing inherently wrong in an educational system that tries to change you; arguably all such systems should: it is part of education to show roles and role models. The problem arises when there is no validation of the self, with the result that the individual does not know how to respond other than to fulfil that role or function. The sense of self can be swamped in a feeling of inadequacy. It has been difficult to extract a sense of worth from those early years.

I have found the therapeutic process of some assistance. Articulation of some experiences has helped validate them in my mind. The process itself is requiring time and space for the self and giving it value. It seems to be requiring a reassessment and processing of the tensions: a synthesis may support a view of self. I am conscious that I am at the beginning of the process but I feel that it is helping to centre my 'self' within the wider uncertain and tension-driven self. It is also helping me to see certain activities not in terms of their utility but simply in terms of what they mean to me, my 'self'.

Kate

Thoughts on Being Me

Some thoughts on being me collected over six months:

I brought my thoughts with me to this house, thinking that I would be better able to formulate them coherently away from the pressures of my everyday life. But I brought them to the place where most of what has become my 'self' was formed: my childhood home. Added to that, it is on the brink of being sold after more than forty years, an event which has the effect of stirring up some deep pools which I had assumed were long since settled and still.

I am also in the presence of my parents. When I was asked if I would contribute to this project I was interested and intrigued. Anxiety set in moments later. It may be telling that the idea of revealing my thoughts about whom I feel myself to be feels like a betrayal or an exposure of those people who were instrumental in the creation of that self through both nature and nurture.

This is not going to be an attack on my parents but I know they will be saddened by any sadness revealed.

A few jottings:

Strength/weakness, rescuing/being rescued
Illness
Work/laziness/worthiness/doldrums
Inertia
Being helpful/good/trap

Trying again several weeks later. I have struggled to do this. There is no point doing it unless I am prepared to be absolutely 'honest' about myself and to do that will be to lay myself bare – to expose myself.

I will start by using some of the prompts given to me by Jenny because I think it will work better to start by assembling a list of features of myself almost at random, rather than to try to write a fluent narrative; rather than being more than the sum of my parts, I feel that my parts are so many and disparate I cannot figure what/who they add up to.

Some thoughts I must set down:

Never being hard working enough to be 'worthy'; always feeling that if I do not push myself the underlying desire to do nothing will rise up and drown me in a swamp of lethargy.

Illness – very mixed-up irrational feelings around illness; that I want to be strong not weak; that I won't allow myself the weakness of being ill; that I won't allow myself weakness full stop.

I know the ways in which all these things are rooted in my childhood. My sister's childhood illness, despite my mother's best efforts, took over and changed our lives. In me it produced this need to be well and strong because that was my role. That was what my mother needed me to be, and it was the role I felt good about myself playing. But for years and years, well into adulthood, if ever I wanted someone's attention – love, admiration, help, sympathy – I fantasized about being run over or shot, or having a terrible illness and causing the person in question to come to me, to take care of me, to love me. *Munchausen* is no stranger to me! And now, when my children are ill I feel angry. My gut reaction is 'Damn it! That's all I need', which is probably what my mother felt when faced with one of her other three being ill or needy as well as her one really sick child. And I have to consciously let it go and relax and 'let them' be ill and then I can enjoy nursing them.

And the workaholic tendencies – the fear that idleness lies in wait – the Doldrums from *The Phantom Tollbooth* by Norton Juster – comes directly from my father. He professes the same fear but in my childhood he was always working – looking after ill people (back to my *Munchausen's*!). He'd be home late and tired and we were to be considerate of his tiredness because he worked so hard and was so 'good'.

I came to the conclusion that no matter how hard I worked at anything, I would never be as worthy or deserving of care and consideration as him, so what was the point in bothering? Not bothering, not competing, was my solution to a lot of things as a teenager. I felt unable to 'be the best' at anything in my family so I opted out of everything they did. Trouble was that didn't leave much.

I minded that my father seemed never to be there and I wished that I could be the centre of attention and not my ill sister or my hard-working father and I felt very guilty about minding and wishing because, after all, I was lucky not to be ill and not to have to work so hard.

There was a lot of fear around. My mother always used to say that she didn't realise how very ill my sister was – that she was glad that my father didn't tell her. Recently my daughter was taken to A&E in an ambulance. Afterwards I said to my mother that I went into coping mode whilst it was happening but afterwards I felt ill with exhaustion. She said (let slip almost), 'Yes, well I was in coping mode for years'. Knowing now how one worries when one's child is ill with anything more than the usual run of things I find it hard to believe that she didn't, on some level, know. She worked incredibly hard at putting a brave face on it but I felt that fear; I just didn't know what it meant.

And I felt another fear. I felt that the world outside our family and our garden wall was a place to be very wary of. I retreated behind the walls of that garden into my little haven but soon came to feel that it was a gilded cage, not a fortress. I lay awake at night straining to decipher every creak uttered by our old house, to hear if it was a man creeping up the stairs to kill me. I couldn't bear to have my door closed; I might not hear him coming; I might see the door swing open. He never came but I was in my late twenties and living alone in London before I rationalised myself out of that habit. I had to convince myself that I could not prevent anything from happening by being afraid; that my fear was not a talisman; that it was not more likely to happen if I stopped waiting for it and went to sleep; that I would not be punished for not being afraid.

Next Session

I seem to be much better at defining myself in relation to others – parents, siblings and children – than just as my own entity.

I am probably happiest or most confident in myself when I'm working. I am able to 'just be' in that context. I am confident of my abilities to do a job or to find a way to do something I have never done before.

The pressure of being busy all the time and not having enough time focuses my mind and I am much more efficient than when I have time on my hands. When I am drowning in commitments I manage sometimes to just concentrate on the thing that I am doing now and not fret about the other things in the queue. But some things never seem to come to the front of the queue and after a while that gets me down.

I feel less confident around people when I am not working. I feel like a different person sometimes. With friends it's okay, though I sometimes find after we've been together that I regret having been unguarded. If I've felt confident and at ease whilst with them I'll worry that I've said the wrong thing or talked too much. With acquaintances such as other parents in the school playground I may feel awkward or inept; with people who remind me of my parents I sometimes feel like a bolshie teenager!

I think – I am told – that I come across as confident and self-sufficient. I find it very hard to ask for help, partly because I expect people to think less of me if I am needy; partly because if I'm just hanging on by my fingertips and I reach out for a helping hand, if that hand is not there, or is withdrawn, I fear I will not be able to continue to hold on alone anymore.

In fact, this has changed. When I first became a single parent my children were very young and it was a pretty desperate time. I struggled to cope; my life narrowed; I did nothing but the absolutely essential day-to-day necessities. I ensured that my children had a sleep every afternoon and I slept too, every day. For a long time I felt that I wouldn't be able to cope if I didn't sleep in the day. I wore the same two pairs of baggy tracksuit trousers that I had worn when I was pregnant because I had no time or energy to think about wearing anything else. I marvelled at mothers who looked glamorous; dressed up/made up. I measured myself out very carefully, bit by bit because I didn't know how long I could last and the task seemed endless: my children's total dependency on me and my being/feeling entirely alone and having to cope and get us through.

But we have come through – 11 years! They are 11 and 14 now and my life is so different from what it was before that I am constantly amazed. There are still constraints of course. I am making myself do something about finding a new partner. For the first years I had no time, energy or inclination. Then I was concerned about the effect it would have on my children. How would they feel if I got involved with someone? I think that the relationship that one has with one's children as a single parent is very different from that relationship in a two-parent family. In a two-parent family the relationship between the two adults is part of the children's experience. As a single parent there is no other adult that your children have to share you with – you are all theirs. Introducing another adult to their world at a later stage is a very different matter.

I am becoming acutely aware that I have been carefully staying within the boundaries or bonds of my circumstances for 11 years. I have not allowed myself to think of, let alone attempt, anything that would complicate my life or make it more stressful, so as not to have those bonds chafe – to be 'happy with my lot'. I have put aside any ambitions, goals or relationships that didn't 'fit'.

Now I'm talking to my children about it and meeting people. But I'm very wary, terrified in fact. How does one start this process all over again at the age of 47?

I've made many bad choices in my life where men are concerned; attracted to men whose lives were a mess, one way or another; repeatedly fulfilling my childhood's prophecy that I must look after people if I'm to feel good about myself and confounding my desire to find someone whom I can rely on to also look after me. I've had to question the 'chemistry' of my attraction to these men. Someone advised me to think of it as making a shopping list before you go shopping; write down the things that you need and look for them and make sure you only get those things. Don't go shopping when you're hungry, without a list, because you'll just get chocolate again and that pleasure is short-lived. But it is hard to manufacture attraction on the basis of a sensible list.

And then there is sex – if I must go there I must. After being a confirmed tomboy well into my teens the transition to being a girl was a difficult one. I spent years feeling completely insecure about my attractiveness to anybody whilst at the same time being afraid of attracting attention to myself and specifically to my body because of what that might 'incite' in men. I wore shapeless, baggy clothes that concealed my shape. I found going out of the front door and walking down the street a real struggle. This lasted through my twenties even when I discovered the power of my sexuality – I could choose to attract men with my body. This was briefly exhilarating but I soon discovered how short-lived that power was and that sexual intimacy was no substitute for emotional intimacy.

When I became a mother my relationship to my body changed. It had a different purpose. When I walked down the street with a child in a pushchair I had a different identity. I was an asexual mother and not a sexual woman and I didn't feel so vulnerable and self-conscious.

It wasn't until I was in my late thirties or even early forties that I started to accept and even like my body. I made a point of looking at myself naked in the mirror to 'own' my body and see it for what it really was. Me! Like it or lump it, better get used to it. And I began to dress differently –to wear clothes that showed the shape of my body and to feel comfortable about people being able to see that shape.

I was in therapy for over ten years. It enabled me to survive the breakup of my marriage and to weather the early struggles of single parenthood. In particular, it led me to reassess who I am, to reconsider my relationship with my parents, children, siblings, friends, lovers and above all with myself.

Lia

Dreams – do people dream in black and white or in colour? I have tried to work this out, but the unpleasant dreams always seem to be dark. Is this because they are unpleasant or were they really in black in white? Alternatively, are the happy dreams really in colour or do they just seem to be, because you have just seen pleasant images involving halcyon days where the sun seemed to shine forever? Many dreams about childhood. These are mixed up chronologically as I am often in my childhood home but my own children are there. Is this because your subconscious cannot imagine life without your children? Vivid dreams, especially those when you wake up and are not sure if the dreams are real or not. When you dream of people who have died but the dream is so vivid that you are sure that you have just seen them.

Fears – so many – so many irrational fears. Where to start? Bridges – I once drove 100 miles out of my way to avoid having to go over the Forth Bridge – when it is very windy, vehicles must wait for a similar vehicle and are paired up before they are allowed to cross the bridge. Do the people in charge really think that this will inspire confidence in drivers? The very thought that they think it would be possible for the wind to blow my car off the bridge… I have never heard of a car falling off the bridge but… Hate driving in the snow. When the girls were young, the more they used to giggle and muck about, the more worried I became. Very tense times and I was always quite sure that I would be responsible for their untimely deaths.

Enclosed Spaces – a terrible fear of being buried alive. Even reading about it makes me tense and if the hero has been caught in such a situation then I turn the pages very quickly. I just guess what happened in the missing pages. I try and think of how to ensure that this can never happen and the only way would appear to be to adopt a religion which allows me to be cremated immediately on death – none of this hanging about in a mortuary or anywhere else for days. I don't really think I would like to rely on the bell used by Victorians, unless there is someone who could tell me it worked for them.

Lifts – I was once stuck in a lift in Covent Garden. Luckily enough I did not know until afterwards that the alarm bell was not connected to anything. I was banging on the door and the doors were opened but now I am left with the dry mouth, heart thumping, counting to ten – if not more – to force myself to go into lifts.

Facade – wish I could be more like people seem to think I am – or what they say they think. They have said that they think that I am hardworking, competent and calm, whereas I see myself as being very lazy and feel that if I could be more organised then I would be able to do so much more. I spend far too much time worrying about what I've not done rather than what I have. I worry constantly about letting down other people and know that if I did what I was supposed to be doing rather than worrying about it, it would have been done. How do you break the cycle? Now that my children are adults, my first thought in the morning is work and, even sadder, the last thought at night. I make lists both in my head and on paper. Sometimes I surprise myself and feel that I sound and act like the knowledgeable person that my colleagues think that I am. On bad days I am reminded of the old adage – you can fool all of the people…

Parent – in common with many other people, I do wish I could go back and start again. My children did not have the childhood that I would have wanted them to have. Permanent sense of guilt, assuaged temporarily when I see that they have grown into two lovely young women.

Home – this is my refuge. Turning the key in the mortise lock is my equivalent of bringing up the drawbridge. Sometimes I wish that I could stay there forever, but then I force myself to go out in case this is the first sign of agoraphobia.

I love trees – in spring heralding another year – a new beginning – a fresh start – everything and anything seems possible. The different greens – how is it possible that there are so many shades of green? When I was at primary school, the school had an extensive playing field surrounded by trees, so that from the classroom you could see the trees and then the hills beyond. Some days the views were breathtaking. I loved the autumn – all the shades of gold and russet. Then the bleakness when the leaves fall and the trees are bare again and it seems allowable to wallow in self-pity in sympathy with the bleakness of the landscape. There is a field at the back of the house and we are screened from the houses in the parallel road by numerous trees. They look different every day and I have always wanted to do as Patrick Litchfield did and take a photograph of the same landscape every day.

Sunsets – in Scotland, the days are shorter in winter, which can make the winter seem very desolate but then there are those marvellous crisp sunny days where it looks fantastic but it is absolutely freezing! However, in the summer, the days are very long. There are tremendous sunsets. My favourite view from my bedroom window was watching the sun go down. It did not matter that it was still only vegetable plots of my father and our neighbours. The fantastic colours of the sunset encompassed all of this.

Envy – I am not envious of people's material possessions or of their lifestyles but I envy people with imagination and artistic flair – the ability to write well or to paint or draw. I can do practical things – I can paint walls, wallpaper, basic DIY. I am a good cook but always feel that the presentation could be better. I love cooking for other people but I always make too much. Many happy memories of family sitting around the table laughing and joking. I am a good knitter and can adapt patterns by changing parts of the design. I can do the same for sewing. But I do not want just to be competent. I want to be the person with the flair to do it from scratch.

Family jokes/expressions – many of the happy memories from childhood are triggered with the punch line of a joke, or an expression. As a child I remember the freedom that is no longer available to young children of being able to go into town without parental supervision. This was one of the benefits of living in small town. I can still remember jokes my brothers told me on our jaunts around the town. Some of them were very silly jokes but they still make me laugh now. Later with my husband, who was well known as a technophobe, there were some very old jokes and old-fashioned expressions, memories of which bring him back to life in an instant; so vivid sometimes that I think that I can hear his voice. I still have memories of painful occasions but these do not have the same power to hurt anymore. They are just a memory that you would prefer to forget and to move on – but when they do surface, they just bring a sense of regret.

Joy – my children – from the day they were born. I was very lucky when I was pregnant – none of the terrible symptoms that some women have – disappointingly no funny cravings but then again no morning sickness. In both instances I was only in labour for a short time – relatively pain free. When I hear of the horror stories of other people's pregnancies, I feel that I have not earned the right to join the sisterhood. In some way, I feel that I cheated the system and certainly when the girls were younger felt that something must be about to happen to them to redress the balance. They were both even considerate enough to be born at the weekend which made things easier in the days before paternity leave. Now when I see my daughters – especially if it is unexpected – I am always surprised that I could have given birth to these lovely young women. The fruit of one's loins is such an old fashioned expression but they are. Over the years, we have made some lovely memories together. I have always enjoyed their company and always feel sad when I see parents – especially on trains/buses – the child becoming restless, the parent becoming more annoyed and snapping at the child, but they do not actually speak to their children. It is one of my 'things'. You would never sit on a long train journey with a friend or colleague and not say anything – why would you do it to a child?

Childhood – are we the way we are because of our childhood or despite it? Many of the things that I do with my children are because of the attitudes of my own parents. My own father was not demonstrative. He would never tell any of his children how he felt. On the day he saw his first grandchild, I was disappointed and, to be honest, annoyed that he did not show any interest in seeing the baby. Then I saw that emotion had rendered him incapable of speech. I too was crying when I saw that, in accordance with a custom that had almost died out in Scotland, he had put a silver coin in her cradle for luck. My mother is a strange mixture. In many ways she is very negative but this negativity pushed each of my siblings and I to try and show that the things we wanted to do could be done. She has always worked very hard and even now in her autumn years possesses the energy of a woman half her age. At one point she had three jobs and of course we had to help around the house. At the time it seemed very annoying but now with the benefit of hindsight I wish that I had taught my daughters such practical life skills. We all have memories of helping in the kitchen – especially occasions such as making fresh pasta for high days and holidays, hanging the pasta on the pulley in the kitchen to wait for it to dry. I can also remember the ritual each year of helping my father make mince pies; the discussions on the merits of the different types of pastry. He liked large pies and was absolutely delighted when he found a recipe which called for a ring of pastry between the bottom and top layers.

Adaptability – difficult to leave her home to move to a new country after she married – especially so soon after the war. People frightened of strangers – especially in a small town. Nowadays there would be all sorts of familiar food etc, but in those days you could only buy olive oil in a chemist! Relations with my mother and my siblings – the perception of each of us compared to what the other thinks. The strangeness of having no relatives in a small town. I could never understand why we did not have any relatives when everyone else seemed to have aunts, grandmothers, etc, living on every corner. Our only relatives were in Italy and we only saw them every few years. I was deter-mined that my own children would be closer to their aunts, uncles, grandparents and half siblings. I must have driven thousands of miles over the years to ensure that they saw them all at regular intervals throughout the years. However, I am very proud of the relationship that they all have now. Definitely a job well done.

My Father was not only a Tall Man but Large – a 48 inch chest – he used to love baking and had his own recipe book with all his favourite recipes written down in his beautiful copper plate writing. In my mind's eye I can still see and almost hear this big bear of a man talk about his fairy cakes.

List Makers – why does it feel as if I am saying it out loud in my head? Should I always hear these voices in my head? Or is it because I spend too much time on my own? Before open plan, sometimes you spent a lot of time on your own – did this start then?

The Joy of Breastfeeding and of Reading Bedtime Stories – guilt free time to enjoy myself. A bit like giving blood. You are joined up to a machine for approximately 90 minutes. They give you a cup of coffee, something to eat and something to read. What more could anyone want? A guilt-free time – how can I possibly be doing something else?

Banish Boredom – buy a book – was a slogan in the second hand bookshop in Burnt Oak in Barnet – fantastic place. I love computers. I can honestly say things like Excel spreadsheets have changed my life – or at least my working life. But how can anyone enjoy playing all these computer games when they could be reading? I think it's the characters. I can always see them in my mind's eye. This is always very difficult when they make a film or television series, and the actor playing the part does not remotely resemble the character in my head. Should they not consult me before they do this?

Small Child – the days seemed always full of sunshine. Memories of the radio always playing, especially on summer days, people sitting out. I have very vivid memories of the girl next door who was some 10 years older than me. She was a teenager in the 50s. I still remember marvelling at the beehive hairdo, the dresses with the huge petticoats and the rock and roll music. I still love music from this era. My daughters refer to this as going to Scotland music as I sing along to these on the long car journeys north. Used to love washing when I was young – my poor mother must have dreaded sunny days. She would arrive home from work to find that everything had been washed.

Halcyon Days of Summer – the weather was always sunny or freezing. Remember fantastic days playing outside – you could always hear someone's radio. We did not have a television when I was young but the radio was always on. We listened avidly to all the serials. I still regret reminiscing with my daughters about radio programmes and admitting that we listened to a popular programme featuring a ventriloquist. People say that children of yesteryear were more innocent than those of today – perhaps not so much the age of innocence as the age of gullibility...

Friends – old friends – ones that you can see once a year but you feel that you saw them yesterday. I am very lucky to have such friends from my schooldays. Over the years we have managed to keep in touch. Four of us spent a few days in Madrid last year. First time, we had been away together as adults without the constraints of husbands, partners, parents or children. We went to galleries and museums and felt like ladies who lunch. We never stopped talking for four days apart from to sleep!

Old Age – awareness of – frightening to think that you may only have a few years left. Should I try and live every day as if it is my last? Are people aware when they are dying – especially a sudden death? Do they feel cheated, or just disappointed or angry at the things they won't live to see – children growing up, grandchildren? Should funerals be solemn affairs? The last funeral I attended was described as a farewell. The hearse was a silver land rover; as was the car bringing the close family. The ceremony was held out of doors. The coffin was covered in photographs of the deceased and his family. It made him so much part of the ceremony and you could not help but smile when you saw all the happy events displayed there.

Memorable Occasions – my wedding, my brother's wedding, my daughters' christenings, my daughters' graduations, my brother's silver wedding anniversary. My brother married my best friend at school. This obviously changed our relationship as well but we have remained friends as well as in-laws for a long time now. On the day of their silver wedding celebrations, they asked me to make a speech. I was absolutely terrified but then I made myself think about why I would prefer not to do it. I realised that the main reasons people are nervous about making a speech are that no one will laugh at the jokes and that there will be no applause at the end. We decided to borrow an idea from television/radio and encourage our audience to respond as we would like. We made two placards – one saying applause, the other saying laugh. My daughters held up these placards at the appropriate times and thankfully our audience laughed and applauded with us.

Pet Hates – I really hate all those advisory messages on goods today. Every handbag, wallet, etc, contains a packet of silica gel stating 'do not eat, throw away'. Why would anyone, on finding this strange little packet in their new handbag, think, 'that looks good, I'll have a bite?' Goods are sold with advisory messages stating that they do not contain items such that the sheer size of the article mentioned prohibits it being in the box (e.g. box selling a barbeque grill stating no bricks included. The weight alone, never mind the dimensions of the box, should have told the would-be buyer).

Oh, To Have a Crystal Ball – what does the future hold for any of us? Would we really like to know? A very dear friend of mine used to say 'Money cannot buy you health; money cannot buy you happiness.' If you have these you have everything. I am not an acquisitive person and although I like to daydream of a very different life, I am actually happy as I am. I have come through the spring and summer of my life relatively unscathed. Now in the autumn years I have so much to look forward to. Changes are faced and accepted with much more equanimity but are nonetheless so exciting – so many other things to worry about. I see the changes in my own and other people's children and now their grandchildren. Will they marry? Will they have children? Careers – what will they do and what made them choose these particular jobs? The changes in relationships and the different dynamics of them as the individuals involved change and mature. On the downside are the debits which come with an increase in years; elderly parents, failing health; conversations with friends of similar ages now centre on very different topics; the realisation that for certain members of society I am already old – the shock of reading about a character described as old and find that they are the same age as me. How can I be old? I have too much to do, too much to see. They say that this is the age of spin. I shall just have to 'spin' myself. Despite the apparent evidence of my birth certificate and the corroboration received by a glance in any mirror, I still feel the same inside. In fact, like Miss Jean Brodie, I am in my prime!

Simon

Or Is It Just Me?

Why are you asking me? I'm probably no more qualified to say than anybody who claims they know me. No, that's taking it a bit far; but I'm really not as well-informed as I should be after so long an acquaintance.

I've started this piece twice. Each time I just set off and wrote until something stopped me. It wasn't a judicious literary critic, more likely a film just starting on Channel 4, or one or more bodily functions. Each time the me I wrote down turned out slightly differently – a slight variation on me. Now I'm trying to splice the two versions together, and I feel different again. Added to that, events have overturned the state of equilibrium (or gentle swaying) which I thought I was in when I wrote both earlier versions.

I'll start with the thing that really bewilders me. Does anyone else do this? I can be walking down the street – on my way to work, say – and I finding myself asking (unwillingly, but unavoidably) whether I am:

- a complacently square peg in an uninspiring job to which I have remained temperamentally unsuited for twenty years; a fact which I constantly fear is about to be exposed; a shipwrecked survivor of a failed marriage; getting by (just) in my relationship with my ever more hormonal teenage children; plodding back at the end of each unsatisfactory day to my poky little ex-council house; with an inexplicably loyal girlfriend and each year having fewer friends and a narrowing range of interests and activities. Is that me?

Or am I:

- a sturdy survivor, in a job where I have risen pretty high considering my detachment (which is a good thing: I am not what I do and I don't want to be); on good terms with my ex-wife, with whom I had maybe fifteen happy years before she became too much herself and I became too much me; a good *enough* father with a sexy, supportive girlfriend; living in a cosy place where my accumulated stuff is nobody else's clutter but my own and enjoying my own company and that of others only as and when I choose.

Which is it?

I can feel my mind go taut as it stretches across polar opposites of being me. Which should I choose, or am I somewhere along the axis in between? I'm not one of the red-faced men nursing cans of super strength lager whom I pass on my way to work, though it's not impossible to imagine that I might have become one of them. How can these versions be opposites when they're basically just the same life from two different angles? Mainly I choose the failure end of the scale. That must be right, because how would I even have come up with this darker portrait if it wasn't real? I'd hardly invent such stuff, would I? It is easier to believe in. My heart isn't really in the positive alternative, though I can tick the boxes. Still, either way, I'm a survivor, you'll note, but then who isn't a survivor of their own history? Not you or me.

I don't know which is true or if both are equally valid. I suspect the brighter portrait is a massive self-justification and I am not fooled for one moment. Am I just too hard on myself? I write all this because this dilemma comes into my mind every day, so it is part of the soundtrack as I walk through the streets. Oddly, when I feel I should probably howl out loud and grind my teeth, the panic is invisible, my face impassive. So I pass on my way, just another citizen going about his business.

I made a fair attempt at self-destruction before I heaved myself back onto the rails about eight years ago, then I held it all together through divorce, set up my own place, did grown-up things like have my telephone number transferred to the new house and hiring a removal firm. I do a good job as a father; I'm still capable of being loved and loving, apparently. If I am not everyone's cup of tea (why should I be?) I'm me, in all the versions; witty, ironic, pedantic, about a thousand other self-contradictory adjectives (I sound like a Charles Aznavour song), and not the least bit earnest, thank God, about my job.

Unquestionably, I came back from a destructive and self-destructive 'mid-life crisis' with my world intact, if changed. I learned some important lessons, even if I don't always remember to apply them. I know in my head the simple answer that the two elements vital to a contented life are being comfortable in your own skin and living in the moment. That's it. It sounds so ordinary, no fanfare of trumpets at the revelation, but try doing both for five minutes without stopping. Such a shame they're both so fleeting, and hardly ever happen at the significant moments when you'd expect them. At those transcendental moments I usually step neatly to one side of myself to watch. There is only one situation in which I confidently expect to experience both the skin and the moment, and it isn't very transcendental. It's sitting at my kitchen table on a Saturday morning with the back door wide open onto a sunny garden, slurping from a large mug of coffee, puffing on a cheap Italian cigar and pitting my wits against the prize crossword. Alone. Well, we all need our rituals.

As for my own skin, which I aspire to wear comfortably, there is too much of it stretched (stretched? More like loose covers) over me and it manages to be both spotty and wrinkly at the same time – adolescence and middle-age at the same time. Great! Anyway, how can I be comfortable in it when I walk into work each morning feeling like the stranger in town who just pushed open the swing doors of the saloon in the western of my own imagining? I don't look around, I *survey the scene*. I don't walk down the office, I *stride purposefully and watchfully*. Nothing happens. Why should it? Nothing's happened. In work meetings I am relaxed and affable because that's how I am, and all through the meeting I am working very hard on being that relaxed and affable person. It is so exhausting, the curse of not being able to be nervous and uptight. Come to think of it, it doesn't just happen in meetings, it happens all the time I am in company and sometimes when I'm alone. I don't pretend exactly, *but I find it virtually a full-time and pretty unsuccessful job trying to behave like the person that I already am*. Is this why I admire the actors who attract criticism because they always seem to play the same part and are always just 'themselves'? Is it easier to put on a false nose and a foreign accent than to 'be yourself'? Of course it is.

The other dilemma, really just a vertical variation on the first theme, is to consider where I sit on the ladder of what I regard as success, between the men taking breakfast out of a can, and those I consider to be swinging from the top rungs, from JMW Turner through to Bob Geldof. A long time ago I saw a Charlie Brown poster which read something like: 'An unfulfilled potential is a terrible burden'. The picture was of Snoopy dozing on top of his kennel. I am starting to get a little old to lay back on top of my kennel and contemplate my potential. It ought to be a bit more *actual* by now, oughtn't it? Preparation is all, but what am I preparing for, and shouldn't I be ready now? Is the great novel struggling to be let out? So write it. Even the bad novel would be a start. I am still waiting for something to say. I used to fantasise about what the blurb would say on the inside cover of my first (acclaimed) book. It would start: 'It is hard to credit now, but Simon was once a civil servant...' in the way you might remark that Henri Rousseau was once a customs officer. Now I imagine my headstone: *Simon X 1957 – 2076 Just Another Civil Servant.* A raven sits atop, croaking harshly. Better get cremated.

Do I like myself? Do I understand the question? Is it enough to say that I wouldn't want to risk being someone else? It always gives me a touch of *schadenfreude* (so glad I managed to work in that word) when I hear that someone who is successful in ways I admire turns out to be a tortured soul or to have suffered some major setback. I can delete that person from the long, long list of people doing better than me. It isn't so much envy of them; I don't wish them ill, I just feel slightly better about me; I'm not quite so far down the queue as I was. With me, at least I know what I am getting, even though not as well as I should.

I am a decent chap. I slow down to let cars into the line of traffic; I make funny faces at children on the Underground (but only if the opportunity presents itself); I chat to people in shops; I feel guilty about not buying the Big Issue, and have once or twice retraced my steps to buy from a seller whose eye contact I had carefully avoided. I indulge in lots of foreplay, often with someone else present. I would really rather be nice than nasty. I *would* go out of my way to help someone, but people don't ask me that often. Can't they see my tail wagging?

I can be sociable, but I feel there is a time limit on how long I feel I can be interesting. If I meet a friend, I like to have a film to go to so that we can have a lively chat, talk about the important stuff in our lives and then I can look at my watch and tell them we'll be late for the trailers. It takes a long time for me to accept that someone is interested in me *per se*, and not in how well I can entertain them or for how long I can be fascinated by them. I am well out of practice, but the idea of going out for dinner with someone apart from my girlfriend, of having a whole evening to fill with conversation, is scary. By the time the main course is served, will we be eating in silence, commenting only on the food and other diners? I only take people's interest in me for granted in the case of my parents and my girlfriend (and most previous girlfriends). How can I put it? I am prepared to be liked, but I can't quite understand why anyone would, and I'm unlikely to really believe it until they've shared a bed with me a dozen times or hung around for maybe a decade. It isn't that I can take it or leave it, but it isn't up to me to decide.

I think I am quite well-liked by a wide-range of people, but I'm nobody's bosom pal. I think people can sense the reluctance I have in risking outstaying my welcome or letting them outstay theirs. I arrive planning to leave; not straight away but, well, quite soon. I read a book recently on how the English behave and there was a chapter on male bonding (even those two words make me shudder). The author ran through the main rituals and I mentally put a cross (as opposed to a tick) against each one: pubs, sport, cars, women, etc. I don't drink beer any more; most sports bore me; I'm not prepared to talk about women that way, however grubby my own private thoughts might be, and I've never been able to afford a car that served much purpose apart from leaving A and travelling hopefully towards B, but it strikes me that what I have against these topics is how they serve as tools of male bonding. Actually, I've got nothing against beer, except that I can't drink it any more, and that drunks are bores, especially when gathered in a circle, clutching pints; I know I was a tedious drunk, after half an hour of being just too wonderful for words. I can be superior about just about any reason why two or three men gather together. The only clique I am prepared to join (not that I have had to turn down many invitations) is that of the outsiders; that non-group that prowls round the office or party campfire just where the firelight fades. We are the group which has no members, because if it did we would risk belonging, and anyway the fire is between us.

I lack commitment. Most of my relationships have survived because the other person persists in wanting to know me. A woman I worked with a while ago for instance. She keeps after me to arrange to have coffees and lunches together. Coffee is my kind of occasion; it ends after a relatively short while and it doesn't outlast my belief in my own power to be interesting. I'm glad she persists, and I'm happy to see her. We have stimulating conversations and I am glad to think she is my friend. I can even forget that, technically, I'm socialising. It's just that left to me we would probably have drifted apart and I would have regretted that, but there would have only been a very slim chance of my doing anything to reconnect. It isn't because I don't like people and I do recognise that I need them. I just don't put the work in, I don't initiate. But I find myself, at the end of a weekend which I started by relishing the prospect of being on my own, wondering where everybody is and why they haven't included me in their plans.

I am a member of no gang, in case you hadn't gathered that. My friends almost all have their gangs, bunches of pals who move in and out of each other's lives constantly. I see my friends individually, by appointment. I am never invited into the gang. Would I join? Probably not. I would love (or would I?) to have a set of friends who drop in, who call out of the blue and who expect me to drop everything and come out to play. But I'd blow it; I'd resent my privacy being invaded; I'd want to stay home too often; I'd find excuses.

The friends I do have (or have had), are Greek, Jewish, gay, Indian, anything but white middle class, middle everything, like me. My office has just recruited a bunch of white, middle-aged, middle-class bondable males and I resent them. Some of them I like, individually; they don't seem so different to me, but I don't want to work in blokeland. Trouble is, I look just like them. I only hope I don't sound like them. I don't go for a few pints, or a chat about how 'we' did in the match last night (we? We?? WE??? What position did WE play?); so we're a bit stuck for topics appropriate to group conversation. The people I do talk to with reasonable success are other outsiders. They are sometimes only like me to the extent that they are not like the blokes, but it is enough.

So I feel like an outsider, but I don't have the differences which mark me out as one. Maybe I should have been gay. I like gay people. I could be gay, apart from not fancying men, which might make things awkward. Occasionally people have said I am camp. I don't believe it really – what's a few extra hand gestures – but I think if I was gay I would be camp and melodramatic and dye my hair a different colour every week, not be macho and moustached. It would be a licence to dramatise. I went to a party last week (not often I get to say that) and the guests were supposed to wear football kits. I went as a WAG, a footballer's wife in a blond wig and Burberry scrunchies on my nylon plaits, sock boobs with plasticene nipples. I had a good time anyway. It was much more fun than being me, though I was definitely in the driving seat.

At some point I fell out of the middle class, although I attend every day as a plausible visitor. I was a reluctant participant anyway, but with my divorce I faded from the dinner party scene. I didn't give any and didn't get any back. Marriage had been a good cover and gave me unquestioned membership for a while. After divorce, I failed to acquire the suburban semi, the people carrier and the golf clubs, and I didn't give a toss about which were the best schools in the area. I never really paid up for the membership anyway, despite going to Oxford and having a conventional job. Those were just things that I did, not things that I became. It's strange not being middle class now that everybody is. Actually, the area where my divorced self lives is full of what I would call working-class people. Some of them live in houses their parents once lived in (and I don't mean a granny flat), work locally and a few even like to store dead fridges and defunct microwaves in their front gardens, something which would really get the middle class curtains twitching. I don't belong with them either, but I feel more relaxed among them. I used to have to endure conversations about garden design, but now if I mow the lawn I'm showing off to the neighbours. You have to be earnest to be middle class (unless you're born at the high end where it's birthright). You have to believe in it as a way of life. It isn't stuff that just happens to you the way I feel life just happens to me.

How do I keep myself company when I'm not making sorties into the speaking world? I sing to myself, quite loudly, at home. I get tantalisingly close to the right notes, which is far far worse than being honestly out of tune, but I assure myself that it is just a matter of practice and one day I will be Robert Plant or Kate Bush. I don't talk to myself but I have exchanges with the radio, last thing at night. I have a transistor radio in my bathroom and listen while I brush my teeth, take my pills, etc. I take over when the radio goes off, continuing on the theme as I go up the stairs to bed. I am especially likely to do this if the final voice before I switch off is distinctive – old, Irish, fruity, upper crust, etc. If it was Irish, I adopt the most exaggerated cod-Irish begorrah accent I can muster, and plod up the stairs muttering to myself. I must be sane because I know this is the first sign of madness. I imagine the neighbours hearing me through the walls – do they think an amateur Irishman has moved in, or do they think me mad? I also answer the questions in radio and TV quizzes out loud, so I know I am not cheating. I can go through a boxed set of DVDs so fast that I start to think I am Jack Bauer or Tony Soprano.

I'm getting obsessed with cleanliness, not so much of the personal kind as the domestic. Standing in the kitchen talking to one of the children, I can find myself running my finger unthinkingly along a ledge, and examining the resulting grey fluff. When I went up to my parents' home early this year, straight after my sister died, I cleaned all the brass handles in the kitchen until they gleamed. They hadn't been touched since they were fitted thirty-odd years ago. I think maybe I have to establish order and cleanliness before I can move on to starting that novel, writing that play, etc. With two children, that day is never going to come.

At least I don't hear voices, so far, and I don't believe in the supernatural, at least not when the lights are on. I don't think we're alone in a godless universe. That would suggest that these gods were keeping us company but wandered off or faded away at some point, and that we miss them. If God wasn't here in the first place, we're no more alone than we ever were. You don't miss what you haven't had, as they say, and I haven't had God. It's our universe, it's the only one we've got and we can do very well without divinity complicating everything. I allow myself to be called an atheist because of all the Theists. I give Them a capital letter to avoid confusion (as with Him). It sounds like a bunch of people who believe in *the*. How can people believe in *the*? If I wrote a few paragraphs about them, would it be a definite article? Bad joke. Atheists are defined from the stand-point that God exists but we misguided atheists don't believe in him. This doesn't seem fair. If I didn't believe in the tooth fairy, would that define me? An a-spiritus-dentatus-ist (approximately)? I think it is the people who *do* believe in the tooth fairy that should be identified as different (well, beyond a certain age, around the time that imaginary friends start to go away). The same should go for God. Oh yes, and my girlfriend sees ghosts. Really. No big deal for her, she just does. I don't believe in ghosts but I believe her.

I know a lot of people who believe in *something*, a higher power. I don't begrudge them, but the higher power often seems custom-designed to their individual needs; it is the shape of the hole they want to fill. Sometimes they fall out with this higher power – 'my higher power doesn't understand me'. When I hear someone struggling with their higher power, I am glad that I have at least one less person to argue with, and I know that if I did believe in a god, I *would* argue, a lot. The trouble with God is that people are always letting Him off, waving away His short-comings. Whenever He, no he, screws up, it is taken as some kind of test for us. Will we blame someone else and come smiling through? Can't he find smaller tests for us that don't involve random violence and ever more imaginative diseases? A written exam would be more humane.

How do I get by without (H)him riding shotgun alongside me? I suppose I have an innate optimism (God (sorry, god), my ex-wife would laff bitter laffs at that, and anyone still reading this will be puzzled, but I *am*. And yes, I'm puzzled too). It isn't based on anything more than that I am optimistic in the same way a clinically depressed person is down. You wouldn't mistake my outlook for wild enthusiasm about Life, but even so. It's no doubt chemical. There's no God, but I don't mind, because he wasn't at the Sunday school all those years ago, just slidey floors, so it's nothing new. I don't mind being alone in the Universe, but I do have difficulties with being alone on the face of the planet. Still I expect everything will turn out alright. Not necessarily for me, not in some of the detailed ways I would like it to, just, generally.

What parts of me am I most aware of, as I plod down these mean streets? My centre seems to be located somewhere behind or in my nose. Not a tickle or itch in my nostrils, but a sort of warm vibration below the bridge of my nose and in my nostrils. Maybe it's a tracking device. It is probably not a significant feature in itself; it is probably more than coincidence that my nose is usually found at the meeting point of lines drawn between my eyes and my mouth, the centre of the senses, I suppose.

My mouth is the primary sensory presence. As I get older I am becoming more... oral?? Perhaps it is the evolution of my teeth from a smooth, admirably regular set of grinders into what feels like a Monument Valley when explored by my tongue: the chip in a front tooth now eroded to a smooth dent (a life of stripping plastic from wires, loosening bottle tops, etc., as if my mouth was an indestructible Swiss Army Penknife); the outcrops and fissures of a life well chewed. There is also the smoking – both the sensation of the cigar between my lips, the ritual and the taste of smoking it; a whole subject in itself. I like the way I can cup my hands round a lighter or match like an L.A. gumshoe. There is also sex, wherein I am very oral, but I won't elaborate. I hate thin lips. I compress and bite mine occasionally to make sure they don't dry up and recede into a tight line. Puckered lips would be awful, a mouth like the top of a duffel bag. When I'm moody or upset my lips close in a tight line and, as my children know well, when I'm angry I bite my lower lip.

What else? I am aware of my hips these days – a slight but worryingly constant ache in the left one. At times I think I can feel a clunk each time I throw that leg forward. I sometimes experiment with sparing the afflicted joint, which means I limp in different ways for a few yards. I feel concern that I am taking my literal first steps down a road to plastic hips. I mentioned this to two much older friends who, it turned out, had had replacement hips and knees respectively. When they stopped talking about their operations about fifteen minutes later and I was able to flee, I vowed to suffer, if it came to that, in silence.

I can feel the tightness of my belt, hitched up to keep my jeans slung roughly below where my 34 inch waist used to be. Women are lucky: they deposit fat behind them, where it can be very attractive (in generous helpings, as far as I'm concerned). Men have to carry it before them where it goes on ahead to announce laziness and middle age.

My eyes are everywhere. Other pedestrians don't seem to be busily examining every face that passes them in the way I am, or taking the same interest in every female shape that comes into view. (I have self-censored this passage, as it became frankly sordid.) Women are so gorgeous, though, aren't they? Who wouldn't look? However, I classify other men I catch doing this as falling within a range running from the rudely unsubtle to the downright perverted. Their eyes swivel and slide furtively about. I see them look at my girlfriend like that. However, I will be postponing judging myself for the moment. It isn't about sex or even lust; it isn't even thought. By the time you think about it, the moment has already passed. There is also the more acceptable game of watching my fellow travellers to work out what their faces and expressions and bodies and postures are telling me.

My eyes are also pleasantly blurred. For most of my life I have had perfect sight in one eye and a long distance soft focus in the other. Sometimes I walk down the street closing one eye then the other to see the world in and out of focus. Yes, I was the guy you passed that time, winking and grimacing at nothing in particular. I should wear my glasses, but I can't be bothered with nose furniture and in any case, it isn't a bad way to see the world. When I wear my glasses in the street, there is too much detail to take in. Recently I've had to peer closely at CDs and book titles in shops, like an old gentleman searching for a second-hand Homer in the original Greek.

I like my gaze. I have a level, intense look in my eyes. Well I think so. It makes me appear to be a good listener. I *am* a good listener, but as long as I maintain eye contact with my steady gaze, I don't always have to listen. I see this focus and meaning in some other eyes, but many seem to have a neutral, impassive gaze, however intelligent or acute they may be. Maybe having eyes sunk in deep recesses in my skull helps me look more profound, but I'm glad my eyes at least give the impression that there's something going on in there. Once, while I was trying to trim my fringe with the beard trimmer on an electric razor, I accidentally shaved off the connecting bit of hair between my eyebrows. It was an accident, honest, but I've kept it like that. I like having *two* eyebrows, not just a continuous, criminal, undulating monobrow.

I don't have a great sense of smell and wandering round London there's surprisingly little *to* smell (not much that's pleasant anyway) apart from wafts from an over-perfumed woman passing by, or a stale whiff of armpit on the Tube. Around my home area, you can come round a corner and be hit by the wonderful garlicky, spicy smell of Indian food, but London is nasally a bit monochrome. Maybe smoking has blunted my nose, so to speak.

I must clear up this cigar issue. I wouldn't want you to think I smoke Havanas the size and shape of nuclear torpedoes. I smoke cheap Italian cigars which look like knobbly twigs, and which I need to cut in half because a whole one takes too much sucking and too long to smoke. They live in a battered old tin, I cut them in half with a Stanley knife blade, and they are tongue-witheringly, lung-achingly strong. Still, I don't drink, so that's something. It'll be the lungs, not the liver.

I think I may be slightly deaf. Certainly I find it easier to hear the background conversations in pubs than the person speaking to me. But how come I can hear what those other people are saying to each other? It's people; they mumble more and more these days.

My brain is full of static. It is a television left on after the channel has closed down for the night. There may be other channels still broadcasting, but my set only picks up ghostly images from these with occasional bursts of sharp picture and short sequences from longer dramas which soon fade again into the fizz. Or maybe it's more like soup, boiling away and churning up creatures and fragments like some simmering bouillabaisse. I cannot think abstractly. I know I'm quite clever, but when I come up with a good idea, I don't know how I arrived at it. It plops up out of the soup. Thought has to be a voice in my head, composing a monologue, preparing a commentary that will never get written, rehearsing a conversation which will probably never take place. The voice comments as it observes me, using my voice. I keep stepping out of my own way, as I witness myself witnessing myself witnessing myself...

One thing that puzzles me is this – nothing is routine in my life. I can't iron a shirt, shave, mow the lawn or visit Sainsbury's without the experience having some fresh element, new people, a different atmosphere, a new texture. If I put down keys, I remember where, because I have never put them down in that place in that way before. The journey to work is filled with new people, plus the familiar ones in a different order. Nothing is ever quite as it was last time. The downside is that when I start expressing myself out loud on anything remotely complex, it is like walking the plank. I don't know where it is going to end or how I'm going to get there. I go into meetings with no idea of how they will turn out. No wonder I don't feel very articulate. I reinvent my own wheels all the time.

Since I wrote everything that precedes this point, my fifteen-year-old daughter has taken 64 paracetamol and survived with no physical ill-effects and I still have no proper idea why – a fifteen-year-old's shrug and something to the effect that 'it seemed a good idea at the time'. Also maybe something to do with me leaving home for a couple of months when she was small? Now she's marched out to live full-time with her mother, and there's no prospect of her coming back. Next, I fell out with my ex-wife, badly and probably terminally. I spoke out of turn, apparently. Expressed myself. So it seems that years of trying to do the right thing and be a good father haven't atoned for mistakes made long ago. No jokes now, you see? Ha ha. Time to stop. This piece can only end abruptly; otherwise it would have to go on continuously, being constantly updated, moment by moment, until I croak. *A* portrait of *the...* what? Not the artist as a young man, that's for sure.

Dannie Abse

Who am I?

Over many decades from time to time I've been smilingly challenged, 'Abse? That's a curious name. Is it Welsh?' Strangers, inquisitive strangers, think it more polite to fluff about my surname rather than boldly interrogating me with 'Who are you?' When interviewed on radio I've had to respond, 'I used to be a 5ft 8 ½ Welsh Jew; now older, I'm 5 ft 8.' A flippant response, yet....?

I think of my father on his deathbed and of the last words he addressed to me. 'I may tell you, son,' he said hoarsely, urgently, 'it's important that each man should know himself.' My father had had little education. He did not know he was repeating the wisdom of the ancient gods, the imperative from the temple of Delphi. Simply, he was passing on to me his hard won wisdom of a lifetime.

'To thine own self be true.' That imperative can hardly be obeyed if one does not have some glimmer of one's own true self. Insight. In...sight. More than fifty years ago I tried to write a poem about a mask-maker. I had him gazing at the masks he had devised:

> To thine own self be true—but to what self
> when to choose is to lose, and all is in
> the dilemma, all is in the not choosing?
> So many great masks stare down from the shelf.
> I want to hear the one voice that is mine.
> I want to know the one face that is mine.
> Speak then, one by one, you many mouths
> announce or denounce—give me but a sign.

Earlier, I had been excited by some paragraphs in a book by

Rainer Maria Rilke, about an impoverished Danish poet living in Paris. The poet observes a woman at the corner of the rue Notre-Dame-des-Champs 'completely sunk into herself, her head in her hands.' The poet startles her so that she turns her head too quickly, too violently out of herself, 'so that her face remained in her hands.'

I could not finish satisfactorily the mask-maker poem but I did write others using the mask-face image as a means to ask existential questions about identity and choice. One of these is 'The Trial'. My father had said, 'Know yourself' so I suppose he would have approved of me writing such poems. Better still, he would have nodded assent to my writing an autobiography which many years later I did (*Goodbye*, Twentieth Century. Pimlico, 2001).

After all, autobiographies begin with 'I' and end with 'me'. In between is the big question mark.

The Trial
The heads around the table disagree,
some say hang him from the gallows tree.

Some say high and some say low
to swing, swing, swing, when the free winds blow.

I wanted to be myself, no more,
so I screwed off the face that I always wore,

I pulled out the nails one by one-
I'd have given that face to anyone.

For those vile features were hardly mine;
to wear another's face is a spiritual crime.

Why, imagine the night when I would wed

to kiss with wrong lips in the bridal bed...

But now the crowd screams loud in mockery:
Oh string him up from the gallows tree.

Silence! The Judge commands, or I'll clear the court,
to hang a man up is not a sport -

though some say high and some say low
to swing, swing, swing, when the free winds blow.

Prisoner, allow me once more to ask:
what did you do with your own pure mask?

I told you, your honour, I threw it away,
it was only made of skin-coloured clay.

A face is a man, a bald juryman cries,
for one face lost, another man dies.

Gentleman, this citizen we daren't acquit
until we know what he did with it.

It was only a face, your honour, that I lost;
how much can such a sad thing cost?

A mask is a lifetime, my bad man,
to replace such a gift nobody can.

Consider the case of that jovial swan
who took a god's face off to put a bird's face on

and Leda swooning by the side of the sea
and the swan's eyes closed in lechery.

No! No! your honour, my aim was just -
I did what every true man must.

Quiet, prisoner! Why I remember a priest remark
that he picked up a dog's face in the dark,

then he got as drunk as a man can be
and barked at God in blasphemy.

But it was a human face, sir, I cast away;
for that offence do I have to pay?

The heads around the table disagree
some say hang him from the gallows tree.

Some say high and some say low
to swing, swing, swing, when the free winds blow.

At the back of the courtroom quietly stand
his father and mother hand-in-hand.

They can't understand the point of this case
or why he discarded his own dear face.

But it's not *my* face, father, he had said,
I don't want to die in a strange, wrong bed.

Look in the mirror, mother, stare in deep;
is that mask your own, yours to keep?

The mirror is oblong, the clock is round,
all our wax faces go underground.

Once, I built a bridge right into myself
to ransack my soul for invisible wealth

and, afterwards, I tore off my mask because
I found not the person I thought I was.

With the wrong mask, another man's life I live -
I must seek my own face, find my own grave.

The heads around the table disagree,
some say hang him from the gallows tree.

Some say high and some say low
to swing, swing, swing, when the free winds blow.

I'll sum up, the severe Judge moans,
showing the white of his knucklebones.

What is a face but the thing that you see,
the symbol and fate of identity?

How would we recognise each from each:
a dog from a man - which face on a leash?

And when tears fall where no face is,
will the tears be mine or will they be his?

To select hot coal or gold no man is free,
each choice being determined by identity.

But exchange your face then what you choose
is gained, like love, by what you lose.

Now you twelve jurymen please retire,

put your right hands in ice and your left in fire.

A hole where the face was frightens us,
and man who can choose is dangerous.

So what is your verdict going to be
should he be hung from the gallows tree?

Some say high and some say low
to swing, swing, swing, when the free winds blow.

The Trial appeared in *New Selected Poems*, published by Hutchinson in May 2009. © Dannie Abse. Reprinted by permission of Hutchinson.

PART III – MULLING IT OVER

(Ages 57-85)

John

Some Basics About Myself

Age 63

Married for 28 years, divorced 2000

Three daughters aged 32, 29 and 26

Born and bred in Nottingham, educated at a public day school, read 'Greats' at Oxford

Spent 36 years in the accountancy and tax advice profession in Nottingham, then moved to London three years ago to take up a job for the government.

My World and Other People

From the earliest I can remember, my world was always very separate from that (or those) of others. To what extent this was because of shyness, and to what extent of deafness (I am practically completely deaf in my left ear) I don't know. It would be surprising, I suppose, if neither of these were a contributing factor. But, whatever the cause, my own space felt sometimes like a cage and sometimes like a retreat. A retreat, because my private thoughts were just that; my own world, where folk in general and my father – a man damaged by his own youth, and only too anxious to be validated by his children – in particular, couldn't penetrate.

And what a world it was! Life's pains and pleasures, not bypassed, but transmuted, from an early age, into something special because of music. My mother was a great embroiderer of stories and facts, but for what it's worth she told me that aged two I was singing in tune, and in rhythm; instead of a rocking horse, I had a wooden Mickey Mouse that rocked backwards and forwards, and apparently I used to sing a song that began:

And what do you know? She looked at me in my dreams last night;
My dreams are getting better all the time.

Music was always the defining feature of my life; I may have been too deaf to enjoy parties – too much background noise to hear the conversations, so after a time I stopped even trying to listen, as the effort was too great – but I could still hear music, and I could sing (the former is still true, but the latter is not to anything like the same extent). From the age of eight, I joined the church choir. We used hymn books that had the full music in them, and I can't remember a time when I couldn't sight-read in both the treble and the bass clefs. By my mid-teen years, with the help of a wonderfully gifted teacher at junior school and a crusty old professional who taught me some harmony and counter-point, I was, in my own mind, the world's answer to Beethoven. After all, he was deaf too! I still remember some of the stuff I wrote in those days; at its best, it was quite reasonable, though not earth-shattering.

But my world was also something of a cage. Conscious of being 'different', if not downright odd, I found how to behave towards other people a constant difficulty. One to one was all right; but the need to find acceptance by somehow adjusting my own behaviour to please these folk, who to me were like visitors from another planet, never seemed to be quite satisfactorily met. True, school, at which I did well but had some 'nervous trouble', put me in a position to know how to behave. And from that day to this I've always responded to people who had 'good manners', and disliked being involved with folk who haven't, or who don't treat me with the respect I think I deserve.

What a joy for this essentially lonely lad, at the age of about sixteen, to come up against Mozart. I shall never forget the effect of first hearing, in live performance, the 40th symphony, with its melancholy, its sweetness, its occasional sightings of victory, its prevalent wild rage. At last, here was *someone* who understood exactly how I felt, because he clearly felt it (and more) himself! And it was okay to feel all that, and, what's more, to give vent to it – which was not what the repressive 1950s had taught me.

Not that that got me out of the cage, but it helped to make the cage a place of delight. But the effort of being 'normal' still existed.

And think of the difficulty of attaining self-knowledge when you feel so 'different' that you can't adjust to other folk. When I was 61 we had a psychometric test at work, from which it emerged that I was among the 1 per cent most introverted people in the population. It came as a surprise – which may itself be surprising in view of what I've said – but who wants to go through life perpetually contemplating his own navel and being all tragic about 'people not understanding him'?

So, as you can see, I learned to manage, to do 'normal' things; to marry, to have children, to give up my musical dreams and get down to the business of getting a degree in a subject that would enable me to take my place in the world, to provide for a wife and family.

And if you're thinking 'Oh, his poor wife!' I agree with you! She tried like nobody's business to get a grasp of what she'd taken on, but it was hopeless. And I really wanted her happiness more than anything else on earth, though she'd say I had a funny way of showing it. Ironically, it was only after my divorce, and another beautiful but doomed relationship with a beautiful and carefree Jamaican, that I really felt free to love my fellow human beings in general. 'In general' is best; no self-respecting female is going to take on an old man for whom the internal agenda (the music, the mental life) will often take priority. But thank God, the long walk through the culvert seems to be pretty much done; I certainly hope so.

My 'Self' Now

I'm not a psychologist and I must try not to rationalise or justify
here.

Study of philosophy tells me that, in the past, some have
thought that the clue to life was reason (Locke). Others, like
Hume, thought that 'reason is, and ought always to be, the slave
of the passions'. Both of these seem to me to be over-simplistic
and intolerable. Exactly how my logical faculty and my
emotional life work together to get me through all that has to
happen in a day is quite beyond me; but I've concluded, late-ish
in life, that unless both are given full weight I am in for a rough
time. And, in my case, it is coming to terms with my emotional
life that has taken so very long.

This has led some that know me to compare me to a child, as
my feelings are very close to the surface and are likely to spill
over on what seems to be small enough provocation. Sometimes
this is so obvious that I act like a buffoon. But, from my
cage/retreat, I don't usually care very much. I tend to take the
simplistic line that it should be reasonably obvious to folk that I
mean them no harm, and would do them all the good I could if I
had the first clue how to set about it. So anyone that takes against
me may have a problem, but I don't. And if they want to set the
agenda, so be it, most of the time; most agendas are not
important enough to argue about (I often say that, as I get older,
most things simply don't seem to matter. But the things that do
matter, matter like nobody's business). To share in other people's
delights is a great thing for me; at such times the walls of the
cage vanish.

I find very many of my fellow human beings very lovable,
and get impatient if others get too critical of their 'friends'. I've
seen too much of people whose self-esteem depends on pulling
others down so that they can exalt themselves. In a world like
ours, it astounds me to hear of people, in politics and elsewhere,
who extol the virtues of competition. Go on, you fools, add daily

to the problem because 'it's your job'! That's been used to justify obedience to the foulest regimes on earth. And we only have one life. Naive I may be, but the cliché, 'it's love that makes the world go round', is a cliché because it's true, just as it's often the greatest music that becomes hackneyed.

Much as I love nature; people, the love of people and the works of people matter to me more. For some years I've been accumulating a library – an investment for retirement, so that I can spend time then with some of the greatest hearts and minds the world has ever seen. And music is a creative activity of human beings made in God's image.

Not, I hasten to add, that I'm free of petty irritation, and sometimes worse. I've already mentioned 'manners' and I have strong feelings about how I should be treated. I also find that 'manners' are a wall – sometimes effective and sometimes not – against confrontation. In confrontations people say things that, if they were truly meant, would convey so much hatred that the relationship would be destroyed. And that's a risk I don't want to take. 'Clear the air'? Pah! What's needed is forbearance, not the kind of self-indulgence that thinks it can say what it pleases and then carry on as if nothing has happened.

For this reason, I don't ask for many people to like me. To ask for liking is to ask for a lot; mostly, respectful behaviour is enough. But, of course, there are some whose liking would mean all the world to me. I like people who I can trust, in front of whom I can 'be myself' in all that self's extravagant emotion and odd views, and who won't reject this odd catena of love, irritability, sensitivity and eccentricity that is 'me'.

And I do find that, for an 'introvert', I love company more and more. Too much on my own means a self-absorption that horrifies me. I've done that, and disliked the result in me very much. One downside of being, on the whole, reconciled to not being in a relationship, is a very real fear of becoming the sort of person who, if anyone asks how I am, spends half an hour telling them!

I'm not a great correspondent, but I think my Christmas card list of personal friends is bigger than anyone else's I know. I do try never to forget people who have been good to me at any time in my life. And, as that life gets longer, there are more and more of them! Whether they respond is a secondary issue; I owe them, they may not owe me.

But there is a dark side. I find that I'm easily nettled – preconditioned, it appears, to think the worst of the things people say. And here the cage/retreat isn't enough; the knife goes straight through the ribs when I'm not on guard. This often happens simply because the logic/emotion equation in the other person doesn't match mine. I do find with certain folk that I have to keep reminding myself that they mean well and the fault is probably with me.

Other things of which I'm not proud: being a very private person, it was a great trauma to me some years ago when my flat was burgled twice within a fortnight. To this day I feel such rage that I imagine doing terrible things to that person if I ever knew who it was. I don't, in the end, want the courts to exact retribution for me. That would be ineffective anyway; anyone who is satisfied with the policing and law enforcement in our country seems to me to be quite barmy. No, I'd want to inflict things myself, to show the measure, not of what the state thinks reasonable, but of my personal hurt. Well, I did say I wasn't proud of that.

Why, at 63, am I still afraid of the dark? I don't know, but it's true. When I joined the church choir at the age of eight, I had to walk in the dark to choir practice along a road that had the high wall of the local prison on one side, and the hugely tall chimney of a textile factory on the other. It frightened me nearly to death. The wall loomed over me, and the chimney seemed, from whatever angle I looked at it, to be falling on me. To this day I feel a frisson of fear if, on a dark evening, I have to walk past a church tower or other tall building. I often vary my routes to avoid them!

And I have a very odd habit; when exhilaration takes over, often far in excess of what's warranted, I find myself rubbing my hands together in rather a Uriah Heap kind of way. Can't explain it.

For a long time, when I was working in the accountancy profession, the sheer responsibility of getting the work done, to time and to the right standard, was a perpetual worry. Waking up in the middle of the night, in a sweat of blind panic, was regular. It felt bad to have to arrange my working life to ensure that the final responsibility went to someone else, and it isn't always possible to get over the message to my present bosses that I don't need, and certainly don't appreciate, being watched like a hawk. But, boy, am I glad I'm not the one that has to answer finally for our product! At least I sleep at nights.

Ah yes, nights. What do I think about? I practically never remember dreams – put it down to fear of going down into the cellar of existence if you like. In conscious life, here are some typical thoughts:

'That quartet of Haydn's is so full of feeling – wit and humanity as well as passion. Bless him, I'm not surprised that when Napoleon was shelling Vienna in the last year of his life, he was out in the streets picking up children and comforting them – while Beethoven was skulking in the cellar!'

'*The Ballad of Reading Gaol*/the last chorus of the St Matthew Passion still makes me weep every time I think of it.'

'Black skin is so much more beautiful than white skin on a woman; if I were ever in a relationship again – which, from her point of view, heaven forfend! – I'd like her to be black.'

'Oops, first of the month again, must remember to pay the rent.'

'I think I'd better revisit that bar of the latest piece. If I were to tweak that chord/rhythm, I could then do ... and I'd love to have it recorded and played at my youngest daughter's wedding. But why have the family who would perform it on Good Friday at church decided they'd go away then? I've sweated away at this piece for weeks. It really hurts. How am I going to hear it and see if it's as good as I think it is?'

'Isn't our way of thinking fragile? Sometimes it's as if the slightest mental spanner in the works will wreck the whole system. How very odd it is that we feel or think this, rather than that? And all attempts to explain it or account for it are completely futile.'

Family means a lot to me. I still want to do everything possible – and more – for my daughters, even though two of the three are in good relationships and in all three cases the 'leaving and cleaving' took place years ago. But I can't stand the thought of them mothering me – which they do sometimes try to do. Whatever *they* think, *I* don't think I'm decrepit enough to need it!

I imagine they think I'm odd. So, I'm sure, does my brother, who is a typical middle-of-the-road Tory with fairly liberal views but a visceral distaste for politicians of any colour other than blue. We get on reasonably well, but it isn't a particularly close relationship – after all, he's 'normal'!

Treasure in Earthen Vessels
I can't write of myself without a few words about my faith as a Christian. I find that friends and acquaintances are worlds away from understanding what's going on here, and I don't imagine that what I say here will change that. But it's too important a part of my life – indeed, the whole of it, really – to be passed over. So here goes:

I said that the relationship in our lives between our intellectual faculties and our emotional lives is there, but it's a mystery to me. But the crucial thing is that it's there. And I find that when most folk want to ask me about my faith, there is no acceptance of that equation.

A good friend once said to me, 'I was attracted to Christianity once (note the reference to a supposed system rather than to the person), but logic took over.' I wanted to ask him – but we have to await our moments for such things! – whether his love for his wife was because in their relationship 'logic had taken over'. If so, heaven help them, in every part of their lives but perhaps especially in bed. No physicist, *qua* physicist, will have anything worthwhile to say to us about love. Nor will any rationalist.

So there's a sense in which most discussion is a complete waste of time; it's expecting God to be a physical, observable phenomenon like a table or a star. Folk say that they can love their partners, because of their physicality; they are physical phenomena, so that's why it's possible to love them. But they can't touch, hear, see or feel God, so how can they love him? Never did I hear a stranger reason for loving, or not loving, anybody. Rationalistic, explicable, earth-bound passionate love! – It would make you chuckle if it didn't make you weep.

But love for someone you can't physically sense seems to give people the creeps to such an extent that they'd rather rule it out *a priori*.

And please don't ask me to explain all the ins and outs of it. Human love is a divine madness, whereby the lover to some extent puts reason on hold and gives himself or herself to being totally taken up with the beloved. Love of God has to be like that, as is his love to us – especially as the explanations can't be given to us; if they were, God would be on the same level as a glass of sherry or a nest of wasps.

Being a Christian is being caught up, despite myself, in a welter of undeserved love bought by, and originating from, someone who is morally perfect – a thought at once completely sobering and utterly intoxicating. And, for all the earthenness of my vessel, it's about being at times so completely full of love (not just sympathy) for my fellow human beings that it's impossible to know where to start, and the greatest difficulty is to contain it.

But if folk want to cut themselves off *a priori* from such an experience, and such a destiny in this world and the next, I can't stop them, because God won't. He is a gentleman, and has 'manners'.

Julie

An Impossible Quest

I have always been puzzled by the question of what it is like to be someone else. By this I mean not what it is like to be a man instead of a woman, black instead of white but rather something much deeper. And the closer I feel to someone the greater the mystery. I can know them for a lifetime; understand their feelings, views and tastes, have a total empathy with them. Yet an element always eludes me. I can never know what it is actually like to BE them and view the world through the eyes of their innermost secret self. And I look at this person I know so well, and see a stranger. Even more difficult is the question – 'What is it like to be me?' Will I find the answer in the past or in the present? (Or does it lie out of reach in the future?)

Through my forebears (a Welsh grandmother and two Irish grandfathers) I proudly claim to be three-quarters Celtic.

Soon after my birth an attack of whooping cough nearly ended my life. It left me a puny infant and my mother told me she destroyed the early, unbearably pathetic, photos of me. In the only surviving picture I am already three years old, looking rather less robust than the old teddy bear I am clutching. For some years I was dogged by a delicate constitution. The result was a tendency to faint which I did regularly during Sunday mass and on important family occasions, which I came to dread (later I was to learn from my younger sister how she envied this 'skill' of mine). We were three girls – I in the middle with an elder sister (more beautiful) and a younger (more gifted than I). My position between the two was not always easy and made more difficult by my being spoilt by my father (my mother loved us all impartially).

The relationship between us sisters loomed larger than that with our parents. Three can be a difficult number and inevitably there was a certain amount of 'ganging up' – two against one. These ever-changing dynamics were orchestrated by my elder sister who had a strong influence on us. A born teacher, she ran a 'school' in our attic and by the time we entered the local convent at seven years old (such a late start was not unusual in those days) we could read and write and do elementary arithmetic. I think too she was probably responsible for our early love of poetry and literature. As I grew older I became very close to her so that when she died tragically in her early thirties I was totally unable to mourn for her – a 'block' that exists to this day.

We were brought up as Roman Catholics and for many years I was devoted to the Church, then I fell in love and planned to marry a non-Catholic. As was the custom at that time, the bride-groom-to-be had to agree to certain conditions which included undergoing instruction by a priest. During this he – a practising Anglican – was told it would be easier for him to marry a Catholic if he were a non-believer. That far from innocent remark started off my disillusion with the Roman church and it was only to please my father that we had a Catholic marriage.

It is said (by Catholics of course!) 'Once a Catholic always a Catholic' and indeed it is hard to shed the shackles completely. Today I emulate Graham Greene by calling myself a Catholic agnostic. I am not quite sure what that means – I hope it suggests my feeling of there being some indefinable spiritual element in life.

I have always envied those with one absolutely compelling talent. Instead, I have many interests – some conflicting. Studying science at university I would spend time in the library reading books on art. I enjoyed sketching but had no special aptitude and the disadvantage of having a very talented artist sister. Latterly I have taken up the cello. It gives me enormous pleasure to play, although a less than perfect 'ear' limits my achievement. In short, I do many things tolerably well and with enjoyment while excelling in none of them. And always in my mediocrity I have been surrounded by talent. My mother was an excellent pianist, my sister a painter, my closest friend a concert oboist – all worlds closed to me. I loved literature, music and mathematics but could see no obvious future for myself. Then the outbreak of World War II drove me into the medical world where I had a successful, although not totally fulfilling, career.

Everything changed with my marriage to a composer. I entered a world where I felt completely at home. No longer an outsider, in various ways I became involved in my husband's work. His greatest love and gift was for the setting of words and our evenings would often be spent reading poetry together as he searched for inspiration. Frequently he would play early drafts of his compositions to me for my views. He always said he valued the response of the 'man in the street' (me!) rather than the opinions of fellow professionals. In addition to music we shared many interests – the theatre, literature, opera, of course and a love of the countryside. He was a keen bridge player and managed to overcome my aversion (based on a childhood witnessing of marital aggression at the bridge table). Through him I became (and remain) an enthusiastic player. In short I had a rewarding life, which was further enhanced when each of our two sons exhibited the 'compelling talent' I had always lacked.

Neither my early embracing nor later rejection of religion had any effect on a life-long fascination with death and the unknown. We can answer so many questions, explore outer space, walk on the moon but the 'undiscovered country from whose bourn no traveller returns' remains forever an insoluble mystery. I once started collecting the wonderful references to death in Shakespeare: 'to go we know not where', 'to die, to sleep, perchance to dream', 'to be imprisoned in the viewless winds', the beauty of the words cloaking rather than solving the mystery for me. For a long time the words of the verse *Full Fathom Five Thy Father Lies* combined with a love of the sea made me hope for a watery death. This was later dispelled when I learned of the slow horrible process of drowning. I decided to forego the 'sea change into something rich and strange'.

So far I feel I have in no way addressed the question 'What it feels like to be me?' I have merely painted a series of portraits and need to dig deeper. 'One man in his time plays many parts' – perhaps I shall find the answer in the many roles I have played.

I have been daughter, sibling, student, professional, wife, mother and grandmother. Sometimes it is hard to believe so much can be contained in one life – each episode alone can feel like a whole lifetime. And the concept of time itself is strange – sometimes passing so slowly, sometimes accelerating madly. I look back on childhood as a time of endless summers. This was a period before the days of weekend cottages, school excursions and mass ownership of cars. Our annual three week seaside holiday was our sole exodus from London and the highlight of our year. Lying in bed at night (hoping the cat secreted under the eiderdown would remain undiscovered), it was the chief topic of our conversation between my sister and me. It seemed we were always either looking forward to the next or reminiscing on the last holiday.

With my grandchildren I experienced the other extreme – of time racing. One moment I was acting as baby-sitter and, almost in a flash, I was being shown by them how to work my television (and being despaired of by my inability to master anything more complicated). With my own children, time behaved in a mixed way. It seemed for long years they were utterly dependent on me for everything. Then suddenly there came a complete reversal of role and I was coming to them for advice and help. When and how did this happen?

Today my birthdays hurtle by. I have left that comfortable period of middle age (where we linger as long as possible). But the idea that I am now an old lady strikes me as almost laughable. I find it hard to realise that the white-haired figure I see reflected in shop windows is actually me. But I am beginning to get over my surprise when offered a seat in the bus and when I no longer have to give proof of my senior citizenship.

I have now been a widow for eight years after a marriage of nearly fifty. The marriage itself seemed like a lifetime but a lifetime passing too quickly. Fortunately, I have never minded being alone although solitude can sometimes give me a sense of unreality and the need for human contact to dispel this. My interest in death persists but this has never been an indication of a gloomy outlook. I am in fact optimistic by nature. When I contemplate my own death, I have no intention to 'go gentle into that good night'. I sympathise with one of Philip Roth's characters who is indignant at the notion, 'that you are born to live and you die instead.'

Have I answered the question of 'what it feels like to be me'? There is a tendency to become the person others think we are. I must avoid this and search for the very essence of my being – that inner self scarcely touched by time and events. Deep down we are always that same person who was child, adolescent and adult, but to find that secret self can be as difficult as trying to capture a lost dream. I am surrounded by a carapace of 'baggage' amassed from the many roles I have played in a long life. This must be stripped off layer by layer like paring an onion. It is a nerve-wracking process fraught with the fear of what I may (or may not) find. As I near the end a shock awaits me. Instead of the expected solution, I find yet one more layer, one more role – the role of one trying in vain to find out 'what it feels like to be me'.

Uma

My childhood

I am one of nine children and what I liked most as a child was when my mum, dad, and all my sisters, brothers and an uncle were relaxing after dinner. We were all in the room chatting and laughing.

I find that over the last few years on both sad and happy occasions when we have all been together, I have enjoyed every minute of it.

When I was young, although I was concerned about what was going on around me, I never used to dwell on things. Nothing really mattered to me and I do not remember losing any sleep, whereas now it is different. Now I am a worrier and worry about almost everything, especially when it concerns the family.

It used to be that as soon as my head hit the pillow I was off. No noise ever woke me up. Here is a funny story:

when I was about 11 years old I accidentally scratched my sister with my long nail and my mum asked me to cut my nail which I refused. While I was sleeping, one of my sisters cut all my nails short and I did not know anything until I woke up in the morning. My brothers and sisters thought it was very funny as I did not budge despite all the noises and their laughs.

Fears, Anxieties and Regrets

Fear: my fear is to walk around in a quiet park, in the dark on my own. When I see other old people on their own and in pain, I often wonder how I will cope with life in old age. I suppose this is my main fear, as I am very independent and do not really like people doing things for me.

Anxiety: in 1969 I had a bad dream which is still vivid in my mind. In my dream I saw a black pig in my bedroom and when I screamed it jumped on my bed and suddenly it turned out to be a baby sleeping next to me. At that point I woke up to find that I was all by myself in the room. I was very scared. Although it was very early morning I could not stay on in bed as my baby daughter was in hospital. My husband had already left for work so I went to the hospital and the nurse told me that the baby was very ill with bronchitis. It was a very painful day for me as I lost my little angel on that day.

I remember as a child when my mum had a weird dream she would always relate it to us.

Regrets: if I upset someone or I have been told off or maybe I have done something that I should not have, this preys heavily on my mind for days or even months. I talk to myself in a numbness way – everything goes round and round in my head.

I am very sensitive with regards to losing someone close (friend or family). It takes me years to get over it – if ever. My regret is that I was not able to attend my dad's funeral abroad and I always feel that I should have done more for him; whereas for my late mum it is different, although I miss her. For over the years before she died I spent all my holidays with her and was at her bedside on her last day. I accepted that she was lost.

A bad time of day is usually when I am working or doing something and someone makes an unnecessary or negative comment. I am yet to come across a man who does not believe that housework is a woman's job! Men are happy to continue the pursuit of any hobbies/activities they may have had before marriage/family life. This does so annoy me, as we have to put things on hold for the good of family life...

Another niggle would be that men are quite happy to watch th eir partners/wives rushing around and will never use their initiative and ask if we need help with anything. If we do ask them for help, then you can guarantee they won't do it properly in case we ask them to do it again.

Good Days

I usually feel wonderful when all my family or best friends are around me. In working life I feel relaxed when I have delivered what I am supposed to.

Sight of beauty for me is architectural building – beautiful garden and scenery.

Here is a story about a two and a half year old little girl: the little girl was with her grandmother in the garden, and the next-door neighbour said to the little girl, who has very fair skin and curly hair, that she looks like her grandma. The little girl turned to her grandma and said, 'Do I look like you?' Her grandma told her that she does. The little girl said, 'But I am white and you are brown'. The grandma told her that it is not nice to call people black, brown or white. She asked why? The grandma said because it is rude and not polite. The little girl said, 'Well grandma, look at the sky. It is white and blue'. The grandma was lost for a response back.

Rob

What's it like to be me? (Who am I? And if I am, as has been suggested, a narrative, how do I recognise other personalities as people, rather than as histories? How do I empathise with a history? In practice I have found it too difficult to deal with this directly; I am reduced to autobiographical narrative. Please draw your own conclusions).

Early Recollections

First recollection: with my father, I meet my mother and my newborn brother, Peter, as they leave hospital. I am not yet three years old. I am sure that this memory is genuine; there are no family photographs.

Second recollection: I am sitting on the wrought-iron front gate, talking to someone. I overbalance, fall off awkwardly, and the latch of the gate tears open an eyelid and brow. I am in a taxi, with my mother holding a towel over my face. Now, I am on my back, surrounded by people and lights; now in a children's ward, getting regular eye-drops, and feeling completely miserable. Other kids' parents are visiting, but not mine. They have been barred: I made such a fuss on their first visit that they are restricted now to observing me through the crack in the door.

Third recollection: first days at school: all very rough. There's an open coal fire in the classroom. Before many days have gone by I have heard, more than once, the refrain:

'Why did you do that?'
'Because she told me to, Miss.'
And the stock response:
'Oh, yes; and if she told you to put your hand in the fire, would you do that?'

It is not far from school to home, just past the butcher's shop at the corner with its ostentatious hanging rack of dead rabbits. It's been snowing, and from near the corner someone takes aim and lands a snowball smack on the back of my neck; it's more ice than snow. I am distraught and struggle home in tears.

Is this the person who is me?

In some ways I identify more with this five-year-old boy than with anyone I have since been. It is easier to love the simplicity of small children than the complexity of grown-ups; but that simplicity tends to return, eventually. Thus, when my mother was dying, I heard myself saying:

'Poor kid...'

She was still my mum, but now so vulnerable and reduced that our roles were largely reversed. It is hard to blame the child for what s/he is: the product of genetic inheritance and the contingencies of up-bringing. From and to what point can we be said to be really responsible for ourselves?

Fourth recollection: we have moved to a newsagent-tobacconist shop in another rough-and-ready part of town. My mother runs the shop for about half the time, with support from my dad and two uncles. My mother operates severe restraints on any potential social contacts of mine after school. Return home late from the playground, or nearby park, at your own risk. Late home, I sneak into the shop, bent double, hoping that Mum will either not notice me (unlikely), or will let me off (also unlikely). How far this explains my regular assaults on my brother, Peter, and even, just once, on my very much younger brother, Paul, I don't know.

Enormously attached to us, my mother consulted us on very little, and engaged in ruthless emotional blackmail. She was also very hard on any suggestion of self-promotion – 'showing off'; but she also trusted (and honoured) me with tasks which today would seem risky in responsible society. Occasionally, the shop would run short of stock. Mum would place a small holding order with a local supplier: typically jars of sweets from Barkers, round the corner; and once a small consignment of tobacco, from Nymans, the wholesalers in town. I would be given the necessary cash, and set off, on foot or by public transport.

I believe that I took Peter (age six or seven) with me on the trip to Nymans. It was an extraordinarily atmospheric place, very Dickensian, both out and in. The people there were extremely attentive towards this little delegation. It seemed that everyone had come to look at us; and, in retrospect, I suspect that they were rather taken with their small visitors (a bit like the two sisters in Penelope Fitzgerald's *Offshore*). This was my first meeting with Jewish people. Had it been filmed, ideally in black and white, this brief encounter would surely have been a little gem.

Holiday Story

During the eighties, my wife Mary and I took the boys on an accidental, do-it-yourself, adventure holiday on Lismore, a limestone island in the middle of Loch Linhe. The hired cottage was twenty feet or so above a little pebble-beach inlet facing south-east, towards the Strathclyde Coast. Far to the northeast was Ben Nevis, and to the southwest, the island of Mull. Our youngest son Chris recalls that our diminutive ferry was called 'Pride of Eigg'.

On the way to Scotland we called in on friends in Bolton, who insisted that they lend us a tandem kayak, life vests and the necessary roof rack (on which to carry the kayak). On arrival on Lismore we found the cottage isolated and idyllic (which is to say that the weather was good), and fairly basic (which is what we, then, wanted).

There were no pubs or restaurants on Lismore, but the general store was licensed, I think. The only general social event that I recall, aside from shopping for groceries, was a midweek bring-and-buy sale at the Community Hall in the middle of the island, near the store. Chris remembers buying a table tennis bat, with a rubber ball attached to it by a rubber band. I bought, and still have, a university foundation course textbook by Michael Chisholm, *Rural Settlement and Land Use*.

With my heart in mouth, I made several kayak sorties with each of the boys to the seal colony on Eillean Dubh (Black Isle), halfway across the Loch. I have no recollection of having checked the tides. Mary doesn't believe that I would have been so reckless, but it is quite possible that I didn't check. Physical danger no longer appeals to me, but then I think it still did. There was, westward across the island, an industrial-archaeological site, a collection of derelict cliff-clinging lime kilns. There were also lots of mussels on the rocks, below. The round trip was only six miles or so, but it involved crossing and re-crossing the tall spine of the island. And as we started down the last, long decline we were quite tired. Unusually, on this largely empty island, we met and got talking to another walker. This was Ken, a Californian engineer belatedly turned High School teacher who spent his summers at the cottage he had bought a few years before. He was very animated about the bags of mussels that we were carrying home for the evening meal. Over a cup of tea in his cottage he regretted that so few of the suburban children he taught back home had had any personal experience of food production, gathering and preparation. Life on the island was more authentic, for him, than suburban life.

On the way back to England we stopped in Helensburgh, and visited JR Macintosh's Hill House, built for the publisher, Blackie. Our elder son Matt and Chris (and Mary and I) were knocked out by the originality of its furniture and decor. We have dragged the boys around many houses and gardens, but this one they really liked, and remembered. Unlike the house, the submarine base at the foot of the hill was not open to visitors, but that hardly lessened the grim contrast between these two examples of human creativity and potential: domestic arts, crafts and repose versus premeditated, mutually assured destruction.

Chisholm's book has been with me ever since. He mentions some long-established agrarian cultures that recognised the limitations of their bit of the planet; and lived, consciously, within the observed capacity of the environment as they understood it. People have not invariably been as profligate as we (most of us) now are. This minor discovery was a welcome counter to Thomas Malthus' gloomy view, first absorbed when I was twelve or thirteen, that war, disease and overpopulation (of which overpopulation is the primary problem: global warming is just a symptom) will inevitably see us off (it is interesting that JK Galbraith, on his recent death, was so shabbily described by supporters of a socio-economic model that is patently unsustainable).

In the intervening period I have tried, insofar as I personally can, through work and otherwise, not to make the world a worse place. But I now have lost all hope for a 'soft landing' for humanity. We are too much creatures of habit and personal comfort.

Somewhere early on in *The Open Society and its Enemies*, Karl Popper writes to the effect that humanity is not guaranteed a happy ending. What is the collective psychology that has stopped us acting constructively on this very obvious truth? Why are we so careless of our children's future?

Fran (Married to Richard)

What it is Like to Be Me

What is it like to be me? Where does one start? How has a shy, naive rather isolated little girl become the mixture of 'me', seen variously as traditional and conformist, the challenger of accepted beliefs or on the edge of the group, confident and calm in some settings, too quick to give my views in conversations and maybe a bit 'highly strung' in others, serious or even prudish, fun to be with...

I was a privileged child; our family lived in large, spacious, magical houses – one even called a palace – not because of any wealth or high family connections, but because of my father's position in the Anglican Church. So it was special – but only on loan! From as long as I was aware, right up until my father's death at 96 years, I knew that people saw my father as special, not just in terms of his role, but because of his authoritative air. My mother was his loyal helper; the magnificent hostess and caring friend; the warm mother; the 'gatherer in' of 'misfits'. I was told how lucky I was to have parents like mine, and I genuinely agree that I was lucky. But of course this was only half the picture. The isolation of the Victorian house in Yorkshire and the antiquity of the palace in Sussex, with its spacious garden enclosed on two sides by roman walls, inevitably led to a feeling of being different. It felt like a special privilege, but also a burden as living in such an environment led our parents to impress upon us the importance of behaving well in company, of living up to a vocation, and the importance of serving rather than assuming any superiority. The downside for me was that being different made it more difficult to feel part of other local groups; going to a boarding school probably did not help this. Interestingly, at boarding school it was clear that our family had fewer material possessions that we could call our own, and our camping

147

holidays were basic and uncostly. Maybe there was a feeling of superiority that we did not need a lot of disposable income to enjoy ourselves, and I fear that this view has continued in me. I really enjoy the idea of enjoying myself in activities that cost little like making my own cards, walking and camping, low cost theatre tickets and cooking low cost meals out of basic ingredients.

If I am really honest there is ambivalence at the heart of myself over whether I am special or whether I am ordinary. I am ambivalent about which group I belong to, which church I feel comfortable in. I do not want people to see me as special just because of my background, and I initiate no discussion on this with people that I meet. However, a part of me is pleased to have the specialness acknowledged if it comes up in conversations; it is almost as if it takes away the need for me to prove myself in other ways – a sort of natural ring of confidence which forms a foundation for the rest of me. If others talk in envy of people living in gracious houses that are way beyond my means too, there is that little bit at the back of my mind which reminds me that I have lived in such a house, even if it was only on loan. Interestingly, when my parents died and with them many of the more eminent connections and friends that I took for granted as a child, I have felt a disconnection from this source of specialness, which at times of lowness has left me feeling quite bereft. Part of this is the natural feeling that I am sure most people have when faced with the death of people who have accepted them in their totality and seen them as special from the very start of life. But added to this is the feeling that I have now become ordinary.

I was emotionally close to my parents, and I certainly felt secure with them. I was the third child in the family; when I was born my elder brother was nine and was away at boarding school; I loved my brother, but the age gap and the fact that he went to school when I was only one meant that it was a more distant relationship. He had a wonderful sense of humour and would create ripples of laughter as he pretended to play the piano on the patient Labrador, pulling his tail as a way of accenting the music. My next brother was three and a half years older than me, and I felt very close to him – more of him later. My mother was in tune with my joys and sadnesses; no doubt experiencing some sense of shared loss with me when the boys were away. Times of relaxation were more reserved for days out or holidays. When I was small, Sunday was my father's workday, and my mother often supported him by driving him to churches and meetings. This led me to feel as a child that I had 'two fathers' – the work father and the holiday father – the one who was a bit distant and preoccupied with work, the other who put me on his shoulders and carried me up to bed, who relaxed on holiday and who, during long car journeys, would tell us tales of two children called Marmeduke and Francesca (based on my brother and myself). Holidays continue to be magical for me even now, and I believe I carry on the family tradition of being much more relaxed and laid back on holidays, allowing myself to lay down all the high expectations I place on myself at other times.

When I reflect in detail I realise that I was a solitary little girl, spending much time on my own with very little supervision. I yearned for my brothers' return from school, and I would write little books to present them on their first day home.

My most poignant memories relate to when I was only four and when my middle brother went away to boarding school. Looking back, I suspect my closeness to him was connected to his personality, but also to the fact that I was left a lot on my own when he was away. At times I admired him to the point of worship. He was able to do all the things that I wanted to be able to do. When he was at home we would get up very early in the morning and we would make cars for our teddy bears – unfortunately his cars always had engines that worked and mine did not. He would take clocks apart and put them back together whilst I watched in amazement. He was incredibly generous – I remember as a small child that he spent all his pocket money on buying every member of the family an Easter egg, and later when he sold his Hornby Dublo train set he spent most of it on buying my mother a dish washer. I have always felt inferior regarding generosity.

So, there was the isolation, plus the 'specialness', and then the enchanted childhood, where fantasy, story and reality all fused together. As I learned to read, I devoured Enid Blyton and Arthur Ransome stories, where the children lived in a child's worlds with little interference from parents. I also loved *The Secret Garden* where the young heroine explores the mansion and discovers the sickly Colin in a hidden room. All these books engendered in me a fascination with finding secret rooms, and hidden passages which persisted right into adolescence. Even now I have dreams of finding a hidden room in my house; this is always exciting but I usually wake up at the point of initial discovery. No doubt there is deep meaning to this!

The house in Yorkshire was a child's paradise. It had a basement which was full of exciting nooks and crannies. When you first went down the stairs there was my father's little chapel. After the chapel was moved outside into the converted old stable, my two brothers set up a Hornby Dublo train set in this basement room, where my older brother poured life into the fat controller and Mrs. Pinkerton, a passenger on the platform. There were also other cobwebby rooms with half walls, and there was the coal store – you could climb up the mound of coal out of the trap door into the back courtyard. In the house, there was an attic which was equally cobwebby; my brother and I made one of the rooms into an icy study and play room. Here we had lantern slide shows with slides from the Boer War which we discovered tucked away in a box; it was here that we wrote our thank you letters at Christmas. At the top of the roof was a small flat roof with a flag pole; it was here that our lack of supervision showed when we encouraged a cousin to slide down to the chimney to collect a tennis quoit. At other times we would put on sheets and pretend to be ghosts; we would usher forth down the narrow stairs and down again into the kitchen where we would try to frighten the two elderly ladies who lived with us; then we'd sometimes proceed down a small path at the bottom of the garden that led to a neighbour, our aim being to scare her as well.

Surrounding the Yorkshire house was a large rambling garden containing a lawn, paddock and woodlands, where numerous rooks made their home in the horse chestnut trees. The sound of the cawing of rooks still takes me back to that garden. This house and garden where I lived until 11 is inextricably tied up with my emotional life, and my sense of who I was as a child. I had plenty of time to enter my own imagination; I could walk my pretend dog, climb trees, pretend I was on a boat swaying on the mast looking over the tops of the trees. My dream was that one day I would wake up and find a horse in the paddock. I passionately loved the garden and wept bitter tears about leaving my soot blackened trees when I was told that my father had a new job which meant moving to Sussex.

I always wanted to do what my brother did, and I did not want excuses made for me. One of the high moments was when my brother's friend Richard told him that I was fun to be with and that if he had had a sister, he would have liked her to be like me. This was praise indeed as I was always striving to be seen as one of the boys (no doubt significantly, my fantasy name for myself was Richard, favourite character in the *Famous Five* was Dick, I loved Dicken in the *Secret Garden*, and now my husband is called Richard!). What I never considered as a little girl was that the brother I felt so close to might also see me as in some way special. Interestingly, this brother was attracted to a school friend of mine when she came home with me from boarding school one weekend, then more seriously carried on a correspondence with my French exchange, and finally married one of my closest friends at university.

Recently, in a training session that I was leading, I asked the group to divide into groups depending on whether they were an only child, or had one, two three (etc) siblings. Each person then reflected on how the fact of being a sibling or an only child had been carried forward into adult life. This proved to be a very moving exercise, and I myself learned a lot about myself when I carried it out later. In some ways I feel that I had a sort of symbiotic relationship with my brother when we were small. I think that at times I felt that I was only half myself when he was not around; I also wanted to do everything I could to keep up with him. But I also realise that when at times as an adult he has not felt good about himself, it is difficult for me to believe his self questioning, as this clashes with my view of him which is deeply rooted in childhood.

My relationship with this brother has undoubtedly had an influence on me; my most satisfying friendships are those where I can form close, sharing relationships, with a certain degree of intensity. This means there is great loss when this friend moves away either emotionally or physically. It has always been important for me to get on with men in an equal way, being able to give and take teasing, being able to spar intellectually with them, and I find I do not want to be seen by these male friends as what I might have termed when younger as a 'frilly' woman (no hope of that in any case!). I was lucky to marry a man with whom I have been able to have an equal and close relationship; we are able to share our values and emotions, and at times I have felt a sibling rivalry with him, and in the early years almost the need to be part of all he felt or did. This could induce intense pain in me when he had different interests which I could not share, and even now, a disagreement of view that takes me by surprise can bring about gut wrenching feelings – perhaps of separation, or maybe at times of having my identity under attack.

How do I feel about my gender? My parents very much

wanted a girl and my mother always told me that on my birth the nurse told her how lucky she was to get the daughter that she so much wanted. However, maybe because of my older brothers, I desperately wanted to be a boy. I was very conscious of the physical differences between the sexes – my nearest brother and myself often had baths together, and undoubtedly I felt I lacked a useful appendage. Often I would dress up in my brothers' clothes, putting my pony tail up in a cap so that the straggly ends made a sort of fringe. I was not very keen on dolls, and the one pretty doll that I was given I converted into a boy by adding a balloon to the appropriate place. I was emotional and would sometimes burst into tears when my brother teased me, or if I had to say goodbye to someone or a special place. Then I would be embarrassed by this emotionality, and I suspect this may be linked with my father's mainly unspoken view that girls and women discussed issues in an over emotional and anecdotal manner. Certainly, when I left for university, I remember him telling me that I had a good brain because I 'thought like a man'. I took it as a compliment at the time but in retrospect I feel a little indignant about this comment although I know that he loved and cared for me deeply, and that in many ways he had a deep affinity with me. As an adult, I am comfortable being a woman, enjoying close female friendships, talking about relationships and making connections with people. But I have never felt at ease with things that many women enjoy – make up, feminine clothes, 'girly groups'.

There is a strong inter-generational pattern of the importance of hard work, service and self-giving, even at times of putting family second. Aspects of my mother's personality reinforced this, as by nature she always put herself in the shoes of other people and wanted to reach out to those in distress or needing support. At times this commitment was possibly too emotional, and she projected on to these others the feelings that she herself would have felt in that situation, and sadly also maybe the deep feeling in herself that she was not worth much in her own right. She lacked a strong sense of self and this meant that she felt it was right to ensure that she supported her husband in his vocation. These parental attitudes inevitably had an effect on my growing identity. There were many times of fun and laughter at home, and my mother in particular had a wonderful and at times wicked sense of humour. But these times were more reserved for days out or holidays. As a child I was very much allowed to play, but the role model for the future was hard work. Maybe in some subtle way one gained one's identity through this commitment to work and service to 'the other'. Deep in me is the conflict between duty and fun, service and selfishness. Am I worth anything when I am not being of 'some use' to someone else – to my children, to a friend or colleague or at work? What will happen when I retire and I lose the roles that define me?

Possibly connected to this is my need to be in control, to prepare and be sure that I do my best. I am at times 'over responsible' in the sense that I need to convince myself that I have done all in my power before I can let go of an issue and let others make their own decision – a tendency which arises from the best of intentions but which can be intrusive and undermining in some situations.

Feelings of intensity usually come to me in three different situations. The first is when I feel a sense of connection with someone through a shared idea or value, or a sudden feeling that there is a shared meaning with that person. The second is more occasional – when I am able to lose myself in quietness and contemplation; I associate this either with complete silence, or with a suffused light, candles, rich stained glass windows, the soaring notes of a boys' choir. The third situation is when I am in wild and beautiful country, and again there is a feeling of connection between me and this environment, either through beauty, or wildness, or through a sensation such as my muscles stretched to the full in pleasurable activity or the wind blowing through my hair. Very occasionally when I walk down the hill near to my house – and only there – I become aware that it feels as if I am looking down at everything from an immense height, as if, like Alice, I have taken the piece of mushroom and have suddenly shot up very tall. This feeling only comes when I am on my own and the weather is good; also only when I am feeling happily self conscious in a way that makes me feel 'all is right with the world,' – an enhanced sense of well being.

In *The Impressionist* by Hari Kunzru, the main character appears to have no fixed identity himself, but takes on his surroundings, and becomes the person that fits in with the culture around him; the chameleon hero has no personality from the past that he can build on as his character is based on him becoming someone else. In Paris he watches an impressionist take on the faces of many different people, but with a sickening sense of personal awakening he realises in between the various masks, the impressionist's face is totally blank. I suppose that all of us adapt to the people around us, or to the different roles that we find ourselves in; does this mean that there is nothing which is truly ourselves? Is that somewhat isolated and shy little girl, the same 'me'? As a little girl I genuinely felt that people around me were much more intelligent or worldly wise. This shyness was accentuated when I was on the edge of a group, or in social settings where appearance, social savvy and media awareness was important. Marriage and feeling special to someone definitely helped build up my self confidence. Now, in my role as trainer, people describe me as very confident and relaxed – not always my image of myself. I am aware that at times it feels as if I am 'acting' as I attempt to get knowledge over in a practical way. But I am also aware that, as a trainer, I am stepping back from myself, freeing myself from any immediate judgement so that I can focus on the 'now'. Later, after the event, I will analyse what has happened and feel much more vulnerable.

When I am in the house on my own I sometimes feel that

without others being around, I am unsubstantial, almost as if I am very visibly 'alone'. It is as if I am worth nothing unless validated by the presence of others. This peak of self-consciousness normally disappears quite quickly, especially if I become immersed in some activity. However, the worst sense of desolation and loneliness that I have ever experienced is during a period of sleeplessness, when for several weeks I did not sleep at all at night. All the well-meaning advice given to me never helped, but only served to intensify my feeling of isolation and helplessness. The recognition that you are totally on your own in life, and also out of control of your own body, fractures your own sense of who you are and isolates you from other people.

Normally, I do not feel that others on their own are 'nothing' if they do not have others around them; this is about me and myself only – an acute feeling of separation and apartness. I can sometimes get this same sense of apartness when I am in the presence of a group; unless I feel very confident of myself, I can often feel like an outsider. I feel that others know each other better, and have a more real and valid relationship – that to some extent I am an imposter, tolerated and not an integral member. This could be in a friendship group, in the church or at work. In these situations I may want to belong, but almost at times there is something in me that holds me back, almost as if belonging might involve some falseness to myself. What I am aware of is that if a group seems to have very different attitudes or values, then in a sense I am isolating myself, as I cannot emotionally commit myself to the group. Sometimes the issue is connected with how the group impinges on my internal conflict over duty and pleasure, and in these situations I can feel, and maybe seem to others, a bit prudish, as if I am being judgmental or superior. But I suppose a more charitable interpretation is that I cannot connect at a deeper level of myself. Perhaps significantly in serious, more 'churchy', groups I often feel myself to be the adolescent rebel fighting against rigid conformity. As a balance, I am also aware of a great need to be childish with spontaneous laughter.

This feeling of apartness can cut you off from a wider view, and I also know that I gain enormously from forming friendships with people who come from a very different background, and whose view on life is very different to my own. In the last few years I have made such a friend, and this has been a source both of deeper understanding and joy and also of much soul searching – a challenge to set views. There is an excitement and intensity about learning to connect with people who in many ways view life very differently, but where there are gleams of intense connection like jewels in an ordinary necklace. Interestingly, this new friendship has brought about in me a genuine greater feeling of connection with others who appear or act very differently from myself – a celebration of difference as a course of personal growth. It is almost as if I have been liberated from my narrow world view and this has been a sense of joy.

I think our children growing up and leaving home has definitely intensified my self-questioning about who I am. With the children around I knew I had a purpose; there was little time to think. My drive for 'duty' was satisfied by meeting their needs and I could instinctively see that part of the parent's role was to be supportive, but also to have fun and relaxation. It sounds ridiculous, but now they are no longer at home, at times I feel that I have to justify relaxing and having time to myself. I also have to work at my feeling of over responsibility. If my adult children appear distressed or unsure of things, it is difficult for me to feel that I have been sufficiently helpful if I haven't gone through all the possible options in my own mind – and who knows, perhaps at times once again risking an inappropriate intrusion into their lives. I expect that as a parent one never ceases to have these intense feelings. Maybe I was right to see the years of responsibility stretching ahead!

I do not always find it easy to 'spoil' myself, and at a more insidious level there has been a slight feeling of envy towards those that do not have this strong sense of duty, and seem to feel that they are fully entitled to spend and plan just for themselves. Envy and jealousy may be normal human emotions, but they are destructive and confining. Someone once explained to me that when you close your hand over something to keep it for yourself, then this prevents you using that hand at all. Age and my faith appear to have brought to me a real belief that I am loved and accepted for what I am, and that rejoicing with others' joy, and sharing with people's sadnesses, leads to a much greater feeling of fulfilment. Allowing myself time just for myself makes me feel more generous towards others, and I can understand at a gut level that the closed hand means turning in on myself, feeling bitter and restricted, whilst the open hand leads to risk, vulnerability, creativity and joy. And of course I have no real cause for envy; I have had a very privileged life, with an excellent education and other possibilities. But at times I have felt that maybe I have fallen short of my potential, as the career I chose for myself (very much in line with family traditions) has not been a prestigious one either esteemed by society or financially highly rewarded. Perhaps I have not carried forward any of the specialness of my childhood? The Christian faith has been a very important part of my upbringing and personal development – but not necessarily in a straightforward way. This was the routine and focus of my family life as a child. In one sense it was not pressurised and I do not remember heavy discussion on what I ought to believe, possibly because my mother had not come from a particularly religious household and, as mentioned, she had a delightful sense of humour. Her focus was not on dogma, but on the need to put herself in the shoes of other people, and be of use (if possible) to others, in particular to my father. I remember her telling me after my marriage when I was feeling a bit frustrated that my career was on hold, that it was only proper that the man should have the priority in terms of his career. There undoubtedly were hidden assumptions and pressures and I was told off if my parents thought that I had been selfish or thoughtless. Boarding school encouraged my independence, but curiously it also intensified my desire to feel part of the family in the long holidays, and a closer emotional dependency on my parents. On the whole I was a conformist by nature, and I was about 22 years old when I really began to challenge the belief set and moral values of my parents and I realised that I must work out my own faith and stand on various issues. I did not find this easy. Throughout my life I have had an internal struggle between 'doing the right thing' as built into me from childhood or as seen by others, and allowing my mind to challenge everything and be a bit of a rebel. There is a conflict in me between knowing what I am comfortable about believing, and what I feel maybe I ought to believe because this is what my faith demands – it is a sign of obedience and loyalty to the God I believe in. At times there is soul searching about whether my challenges arise from intellectual arrogance, and a refusal to give up the self-centred bits of myself, which can go contrary to another belief that giving myself up and letting God's spirit work through me will help me become fully human in the richest sense of the word. I am clear there is a value in continually searching for the pearl of great price. More confusing to me is the fact that some of my beliefs go contrary to what others see as approved doctrine and biblically based. I instinctively feel that a certain sort of doctrine is wrong and leads to oppression and discrimination. Possibly those of my close friends who do not have a faith will see this as a self imposed conflict and burden, but I sincerely believe that there is a spiritual dimension, and that being connected to God is the best way to heal the terrors and selfishness around us in the world and in ourselves. And I do not believe that those feelings that arise from my depths are always those that I should act on. Hence, the tension between the need to use my mind to question and the need to accept some things on faith. But what I can acknowledge at a deep level is that many of the great theological truths are grounded on psychological truths; that those who only live for themselves or put material possessions at the pinnacle of their life, who envy or feel unable either to ask for forgiveness or forgive others, do not inspire me or convince me that they are living fulfilled lives.

Maybe the struggle between being conformist as well as being real to myself has meant that I have never had the confidence to be really original or launch out in my own strength. I have a good mind, but it is more derivative than original – it is about putting together other people's ideas and making sense of them. I am able to put my views forward, and can feel very strongly about something, but only if I am well versed in the subject. This means that I can verge from being seen as very outspoken and maybe even a bit strident in giving my view, to being conventional or withdrawn when I do not want to be marked out in the group or to upset people by saying something contrary. As I grow older I am becoming more confident that it is alright to be different; the more I believe that I am worth something in myself, then the easier it becomes to accept being different not as a criticism of myself but as a fact of life and maybe even something to celebrate.

When I was first asked to reflect on myself I felt that there was nothing to say. Analysing feelings and attempting to put them into words can sometimes give the self questioning and negative feelings a greater prominence than is actually true. The analysis neglects to include what I am proud of – my relationship with my husband and children, my enthusiasm, my ability to energise people and be empathic with them, and my enjoyment and skills at connecting with people in a work setting. Interestingly, my time of reflection seems to have validated to myself that it is alright to be me, to be different or to be on the fringe of a group. It has helped me realise how much of my thoughts are similar to the thoughts of others as they come to terms with who they are, and that the self-consciousness that I can feel when on my own is just one aspect of being a human being. And if my thoughts are not the same, then that is also alright. Moreover, from a religious point of view, I am also feeling more loved and accepted for who I am, which frees me up to be myself and takes away the need to always be proving that I am 'doing the right thing' or having 'correct beliefs'.

Richard (Married to Fran)

A Mass of Contradictions

The very idea of writing this goes against the grain. Two themes have followed me throughout my life. First, don't focus on yourself – it's ever so self-indulgent and (almost) sinful. This has got to me, even to the extent that I have never really allowed myself to spend time thinking about the past. Being nostalgic is just 'not me'. I cannot allow myself to look at old photos just for the sake of bringing back the memories. I have to do it with someone else so there is a 'purpose' to it.

I have put off starting this because I am so uncomfortable with the idea of spending precious time on me without any apparent outcome. Why should anyone want to read my verbal dribbles?

But I have made a start and, just maybe, the very process of writing will help me to get over (or at least understand better) this particular hang-up.

The other theme is that whatever you present to the outside world – whether it be verbal, written or musical – it says something important about you; it is you in that moment. And once out it cannot be erased, retrieved or altered. It is there forever. I therefore have lived in fear of presenting anything that does not truly represent me, or the very best that my brain/mind/soul can produce. I cannot write a letter without doing at least three drafts. I cannot speak in a meeting or social gathering without having thought through what it is I really mean. I cannot play music in public unless I have practiced to as near perfection as I can get it. So to be asked not to look over what I have written or chuck anything, feels like asking me to go against my very nature (there, I have just altered that phrase already. This is going to be very difficult).

And yet... And yet. I have chosen a career – social work – that has required me to go into my background, to understand what makes me tick. I have married someone who is very perceptive and articulate about feelings and talking with her about emotions and why we behave as we do have been some of the most rewarding times in my life. Also for the past 12 years I have kept a diary as part of a daily 'quiet time'. I find God communicates best with me through my feelings and daydreams, as well as the coincidences of daily life. Writing these thoughts down reinforces my listening skills. I have done, and still do, a lot of self-analysis and find it very satisfying, yet I start this exercise saying I hate focusing on me.

What do I really mean? I really am a mass of contradictions. But that is perhaps a helpful starting point. All my life I have tried to make sense of things. I was attracted to social work because I wanted to understand why people (young offenders at the time) behaved the way they did, and then help them change their ways. My wife Fran and I speak endlessly about why we behave the way we do, and after meeting up with friends often discuss why they behave as they do, not as a character assassination exercise but to try to understand behaviour. At work I have a real gift for writing up long and complicated discussions in a way that makes sense of all that has been said. I am fixated at the moment with faith and read avidly about the different strands of the 'faith movement' – not just organised religions – because I want to be able to find the common denominator that makes all the apparently conflicting ideas make sense.

So, perhaps this exercise is permission for me to accept I am a mass of contradictions and not to have to worry about it, or try to make sense of it. That feels like being let out of a cage with unlimited freedom to roam. I hope I have the courage to make use of the freedom and don't crawl back to safety too soon.

'I am Special'

I am a great believer in the internal tape that gets produced during your early years and which you constantly replay to yourself throughout life, each playing reinforcing the message more strongly. A dominant message on my tape is that 'I am special' – special, I guess because I was the only child born of parents in their late 30s who had never expected to get married let alone have a child; special because I showed musical gifts at a young age and that was important to parents who were both keen amateur musicians. One of the high spots was going in to the London Musical Competition Festival (a prestigious London-wide competition) at the age of eight and winning a cup with a 100 per cent mark; something the adjudicator had never done before. I went on to win a number of other competitions in the next four years, and was one of the star pupils of a first class teacher, playing in her annual pupils' concert at the Wigmore Hall alongside people who were to become soloists and professors at the colleges of music. Special because I became head boy of my primary school, went to a public school, went to university and then did an MA in Canada – in a family where no one had passed their 11+ or achieved any O levels. Special because I found my way up the management tree, almost despite myself, becoming Assistant Area Director of Social Services at the age of 41 in Surrey, in a family where no one had any 'status' or professional role. Special because I married a bishop's daughter and got married in a cathedral. For a family that lived in the shadow of Lord Salisbury up the road in Hatfield House (my uncle was his fishmonger, and an aunt was a maid to Lady Salisbury), it was as if I had joined the aristocracy.

'He Can Do Anything if He Puts His Mind To It'

My mother repeated this quote to me from one of my cousins, with obvious pride. That's one of the great benefits of feeling special. In whatever situation I am in, I must believe that I can do something that others cannot do and then do it. If I look back on my work career, I am never happier than when I am stretching the boundaries of the current job, dreaming of new ways of doing things, and then throwing myself into the detail of making it happen. The times of greatest depression have been when I am stuck in a role where I cannot make any difference, or where control has been taken from me. In social life, I cannot bear to be peripheral. My most treasured moments are where I have been really valued for the person I want to be – someone special. In situations, even now, where I think I am not valued I will opt out and almost deliberately turn my back. It is me that has decided not to belong, to avoid the pain of the reality, which is that this company does not see me as anything special.

But there are other parts of my internal tape that directly undermine this drive to be special (those contradictions again). 'Never argue, you are likely to destroy people,' – never said in so many words, but a powerful belief that my mother in particular instilled in me. As a family we never discussed anything of importance. When I took Fran home to meet my parents I got into a heated discussion with Dad about education over the dinner table. My mother took Fran aside and said to her, in a panic, 'you must stop them'. Why, they are enjoying themselves? 'But it's so rude'. Despite all those years at university, at work, enjoying the company of friends who are incredibly articulate and enjoy arguing about everything, I still cannot erase that tape message and still feel totally incapable of entering freely into a debate. The tape is still telling me it's rude and potentially destructive. I still cannot accept it when people say that I make a contribution, whether at work or in social gatherings. The image of me as being quite unable to express my views remains dominant.

'Never Put Yourself Out, Just Be Happy'

When I look back, I cannot recall my parents striving for any goal for themselves. My father was an accounts clerk and remained in the same job throughout married life. My mother was content to stay at home as a housewife; her social life was other members of her family living in the same town, plus her next-door neighbour. They never looked for any friends outside this circle. If anything became an effort, the rule was to withdraw and not put yourself out. In later life, when she came to stay with me when we had young children, she could never understand why Fran and I were always on the go, pushing ourselves to the limit with family, work, social and church engagements. She felt almost upset – and rightly so as, no doubt, her expectation was that the world should revolve round her when she came, because that was the expectation within her own family. All my life I seem to have been driving myself to the limits of my mental and bodily abilities. I have never known where that has come from. But I now think it must have come, in part, from a reaction to this philosophy. I have tended to distance myself from my family – seen them as a little beneath me – and I have often said to Fran, 'I don't want to get like my parents'. Maybe what spurs me on to give myself new targets all the time is the fear that I will sink into the endlessly repetitive and unadventurous way of life that I have characterised (unfairly) as being 'home'.

'I Am Not Like Other Boys'

Never a statement made by anyone else, but one I have often made to myself in life. Where did it start? I have always been a sensitive child. I remember when I was very young, my mother used to bribe me with money to encourage me to stand up to my friends in a fight. I would be strong enough to pin my friend down but I would still be crying as I was doing it. I don't think it was to do with losing or being afraid, I just hated combat in any form. Then there was my music. I started piano and violin when I was five and this required me to practice about one hour per day. I remember occasions when friends were playing in the road outside the front room where the piano was, and my mother pulling the curtains so I would not be distracted. I don't recall being upset by this, and I certainly enjoyed, and was good at, football but it did mark me out as being different. I can even remember at university feeling almost ashamed at carrying my violin case around in public. To me it marked me out as being effeminate.

Other random thoughts on this theme: I have always enjoyed the company of women more than (most) men. Indeed I seem to have chosen interests and a career that bring me into contact with women more than men: music, social work, church. Recently a group of men in our neighbourhood starting meeting up for a drink and chat; their talk was all cars, model trains, swapping travel information, a bit of football. I felt I had nothing in common. With women it tends to be much more interesting: more people-centred, talking of feelings and ideas. When women found me attractive, it was usually because of my outward looks (some say I was handsome then!), my music, my relaxed nature and the fact that I was interested in them as people not because of my maleness. Sex was not primarily about male assertiveness and getting my oats, but about enjoying the sensuousness of the human body and giving pleasure to the other person.

A lot of my drive, however, seems to be an attempt to demonstrate to myself that I really am a man. As a child I used to have endless daydreams about leading men in battle, being a hero rescuing maidens from dungeons, being the leader in everyday situations in my life. When I grew up I was never satisfied with myself. The driving message was, 'I am not the sort of person that can take responsibility'. I became a Team Manager – but when I had proved that I could take this responsibility I convinced myself that this was not real responsibility, I could only prove this by being in my boss's shoes. So I got his job, but after four years, convinced myself that this proved nothing. So at 41 I became an Assistant Director. I probably did a good job (at one stage and was being groomed to be a Director) but even then I convinced myself that other colleagues were better able to handle responsibility than me.

But by the time I reached 50 something catastrophic had happened. It was as if the bottom had dropped out of my life. I had no energy, no ability to put a sentence together, no joy in life, a profound feeling of inadequacy and ineffectiveness, as if I was an invisible person in any social/work gathering, and suffered from impotence. It was almost as if the loaded spring that had propelled me into achievements up until 40 had inexplicably wound down, never to return.

At 45 I was diagnosed with hypothyroidism, and one of the well known symptoms is a total lack of energy and feelings of depression. It also coincided with a time of turbulence at work. I had joined a good management team and we had worked hard to build our department. Then we had to reorganise and I felt really devastated when all my colleagues left and I joined another team as a complete stranger. Then there was this perennial feeling that I should not be in a position of responsibility and that sooner or later I would be found out. It was as if I could no longer live that lie. I had even thought of giving up work and becoming a barman, because that would make me feel more comfortable with the image I had of myself. Is this man's mid life crisis? At the time I did not even think of that. I just considered I was the only person in the world who felt quite so inadequate, and I dare not expose my real self to anyone.

It also brought me into headlong collision with all those messages that 'I am special'. The painful truth was that I had been living a lie – the tape had been wrong all the time – I was definitely not special. The memory that really captures this was around my 50th birthday. I really felt I was going to die at this time, and subconsciously was preparing myself for it. When Fran asked what I wanted for by birthday I said a music evening playing with some friends. I can remember thinking that when I am dead people will at least remember me for my piano and violin playing. Otherwise they will have nothing to remember me for – nor will my family.

I have gone into this period, not only because it so shook me, but also because it provided the springboard for the journey I have travelled since.

It is trite to say a religious conversion saved me (I don't like that kind of terminology and it is not true because I did have a faith beforehand). But what I did, in despair, was to throw myself onto God, admit that I was foolish ever to believe I could do anything on my own, and cried out for some relief from the feelings of despair. I never expected anything to happen; it was impossible to believe that anyone or thing could get me out of it. Over the next three to four years I experienced a very painful and tortuous journey. Now it's like I have climbed up a mountain, reached a peak and can look back at the path I have trodden. From this vantage point I can see that my feelings of specialness were so ingrained that nothing short of a total collapse of self-belief would have forced me to a true humility, borne of experience, and the recognition that to really live you must be totally reliant on God. That strange paradox – to truly live you must give up yourself.

So, I now see myself as special once more, but not because of anything I have achieved or need to achieve in future but because God sees me as special. That takes all the pressure off me, because in the end the only person I need to impress is Him-above not anyone else. If you believe that God gave you talents and personality for a purpose, then you don't need to spend time berating your lack of talent, just enjoy being yourself (a far cry from my former preoccupations with proving myself all the time and trying to fit into a mythical 'male' image).

Three years ago I took on a project of sorting out the home care service in Surrey. There were ten managers managing over 700 staff who had been ignored by the service, felt demoralised and lacking in self-worth. I did not line-manage them so could not provide the normal leadership role or make decisions for their managers. I found myself turning all the normal management practice and theory on its head. Instead of focusing on the outcomes, getting managers to focus on their targets, and being 'managerial', I found myself just wanting to love them. I would spend time thinking of their particular situation, allow myself to take on board their feelings, and go into meetings just focusing on loving them. There were some very tough moments, and many times when I thought I had lost their respect with my non-assertive approach, but always in prayer time came the message – leave the outcomes to me, you just concentrate on loving them. The amazing thing is that after three years all the targets have been achieved, managers are much more confident and assertive and I truly believe they think they have done it themselves (equally amazing, I don't *mind* that they think they have done it all on their own even though I know I played a large part in making some things come together).

It feels like an extraordinary transformation – someone who had been obsessive about being in control, now willing to let go and allow situations to unfold, just trusting that things will turn out okay. A quote from *Conversations with God*:

There are only two emotions – fear and love... Fear is the energy which contracts, closes down, draws in, runs, hoards, harms. Love is the energy which expands, opens up sends out, stays, reveals, shares, heals, closes down.

I would add that fear is the energy that needs to control. Love relinquishes control.

Someone who has always shied away from powerful feelings – especially pain and anger – now learning to welcome and stay with them. I sometimes feel I am most 'me' when I am being alongside and entering into others' powerful feelings. I read a book last year about someone who found himself 'called' to be an intercessor. He had to purge himself gradually of all ego and devote himself to others, spending long periods of time praying and staying alongside individuals. The reward was an incredible life of seeing people changed, healed, new projects being set up which were considered impossible. In my higher moments I think this is how I would like to live the rest of my life.

But of course I don't live my life entirely in these higher moments. The old self is always present and continually intrudes. The all-too-human bit of me still sees 'me' as the centre of my life, very much wants to be approved for the things I have achieved, is very self-conscious, always wondering what others are thinking of me (usually assuming the worse), sees little hope that anything will change much for the better (in terms of society or improvements in the Developing World) and clings to hope in desperation rather than expectation.

Final thoughts on my children – the greatest (unexpected) bonus in my adult life apart from Fran: Because I had never discussed anything with my parents, and had wanted to distance myself from them as soon as I got to university, I fully expected my children to do the same. It is a constant source of amazement that they seem to enjoy talking to me, seem to value my comments, are able to accept me as I really am and don't judge me for all my failings. Marrying into Fran's family was a pleasant shock: I became part of a family that was close and seemed to share everything. But these past few years have, for me, been the first time I have experienced what it is really like to be part of a family.

When I was younger my puritan work ethic was so strong that I felt it was wrong to put family before work, and Fran has many embarrassing stories when this rebounded on the family, like when I was the Principal social worker at St Helier Hospital and Fran went into St Helier to have Christopher. During the long labour I went to have lunch with members of my team downstairs and spent so long talking work I almost missed the birth. It also seems a terrible thing to say but I almost felt guilty when I enjoyed being with the family, as if I shouldn't be enjoying myself. This was maybe a result of working with people who had such a bad experience of families and never seemed to have felt contentment, let alone happiness, or it was something deeper within me.

Now I feel freed up from any sense of duty. I want to put family first. My greatest delight is seeing Fran working full time and throwing herself into work. Each year I give myself some targets. For the past few years one has been to support Fran in her work – I have had my career, and I want to make sure Fran can enjoy hers (even if it is a little later in life). I also want to give time to thinking, praying about the children and, if asked, giving them time.

Helen

Early Years

As a young child I used to feel I was looking out on to the world as through a window. Every so often this would spill over into the odd sensation that I did not understand who or what it was on this side of the window and I would doubt my own material existence. Although it felt quite unreal, I would have no sense of looking down on myself or being 'out of body', just puzzled as to where I fitted in to the scheme of things. This would happen quite frequently, but it fell away by late childhood so that now I can evoke it only if I try very hard. This primitive consciousness from childhood has been lost to my adult inner world, which looks as much inwards as out.

My inner world, my memories, are getting into a muddle. There are too many of them to organise anymore and trying to construct any continuous story from them has proved impossible, so I must make the best of what offers itself. Even then I am not sure where my early memory is true or where it has been jogged into action by photographs. I have a great many snatches of memory from about the age of three onwards, but they only settle into a coherent narrative from the age of five or six.

My first home was in Welwyn Garden City. My recollections are of pretty red brick houses, just like dolls' houses, lots of trees and wide green verges. The sun is always shining in my memories, which must be a good thing. My very first memory, and I am sure it is true, is of being in my pram in the covered vestibule of Welwyn Department Stores. Babies were left there whilst their mothers shopped, an action that would be considered a crazy risk today. I remember later having the freedom to play up and down the street with Robin and Freddy, my two friends from the same road. I remember also watching a red squirrel with my father in the little patch of woodland at the end of our street. Another sunny memory from early years is of walking along the edge of a field of ripe wheat with my grandmother, on a visit to Sussex. When I was seven, my baby sister was born and shortly afterwards my father's work relocated to the north, to Harrogate, and we left at Christmas. Looking out from the taxi taking us with our luggage to the station, I saw Robin in the street holding a large stick, one end on the ground. He was standing on one leg and had the other twisted round the stick, and even then it seemed poetic.

Harrogate was a huge contrast to the life I had known. The town was much more spacious and noticeably cooler. Most of the houses were built of northern stone darkened with age, large and imposing. Our house, more newly built of stone that was still grey in colour, was also on a much larger scale than we had had before. Nothing ever seemed so cosy again after the move. But Harrogate had plenty going for it, and all the creature comforts were there. I had outings into town with my mother, always well-dressed for the occasion, for tea at Betty's tearoom, or sometimes I would go with her to Marshall and Snelgrove when she met her other ladies for their regular morning coffee and I would get terribly bored.

My parents were second generation, both children of refugees from Eastern Europe who had come to Britain at the beginning of the nineteenth century to escape persecution and a hopelessly limited future. Both my parents in turn benefited from the opportunities that this country gave them, especially for a high quality, free education up to university level, and this was something they were always aware of.

As one of a large family living in genteel poverty, my mother did not have a particularly easy childhood. Her father was almost blind for many years because of cataracts, and I am not sure how much he was able to work, and then he died at the age of forty-five when my mother was in her teens. In adulthood she was a strong character, full of love and good ideas, fun to be with but self-centred. She was intellectual but not organised enough, so that her conversation could jump around unpredictably. I was scared too by her inconsistent moods and actions, as she flitted between joy and anger. I never quite knew where I stood with her, but fortunately her capacity for affection always just managed to counterbalance the bad times. Only when I became an adult could I see how her background and her many hard life experiences had influenced her behaviour, and judge her less.

My father, by contrast, was gentle and unfailingly good-natured, radiating an almost tangible warmth. He, too, had a razor-sharp scientist's brain and interests that ranged from opera to politics, hill walking and photography. He was the stable point in our household. I have a single memory of him getting irritable, but it came only at the end of a long hot day of driving in France with a fractious family in the back of the car. If my picture of him is idealised, I can only say in my defence that the few people still around to remember him all carry the same image.

My sister was a small baby when we moved to Harrogate. My memories of her are fragmented, of my mother holding her up to the window of the nursing home in Welwyn soon after her birth for me to see her (as children were not allowed to visit) and I also remember helping to look after her, fetching nappies and the like. Our pretty baby had silky dark curls and a face in my father's mould, and she did all the right things at the right time and was dearly loved. There was a large black and white photograph of her taken a little later by my father, in profile and standing on her tiptoes to reach some object across the top of a desk. These are the things I remember. She died when she was eighteen months old, when the neck ribbon of her nightdress caught on the protruding knob on the rim of her drop-side cot. What I remember as yesterday is the devastation of the whole family, my parents at my bedside the next morning waiting for me to wake so they could impart the news, my mother going wild with grief and guilt, my father and grandparents in their distress, and my own. It is to my parents' credit that they did not try to exclude me from what was going on and, at eight, I was fully aware of the impact. Nor could they shield me and I raged at the loss and waste.

A little over a year on from this catastrophe we had the best of endings when my mother, now aged forty-two, gave birth to twins, a boy and girl. I had a family again and we could all now let things move on. I remember the blur of activity when they arrived, the excitement and the bewilderment as they turned my parents' early middle age on end. However much joy they brought they were also unmitigated hard work, so hard in fact that my mother resorted to live-in help for the first few years – Yorkshire girls who wore green nylon uniforms with white elasticated arm cuffs and were tough-minded but dedicated to the twins. One of these girls had a Polish boyfriend twenty years her senior, who would visit. He had been a prisoner of war and had a stock of exciting stories about his wartime exploits. He was rather good looking and decidedly romantic. I heard afterwards that they married but it had not worked out and, considering the culture gap, it is not surprising.

Life at home now went on in a rather satisfactory way. The twins flourished and my parents settled into a contented provincial way of life. We got our first car – an air force blue Morris Minor – which we all piled into at weekends and had outings into the spectacular Yorkshire countryside around us. My father was far keener on walking than my mother and quite often she would stay in the car with a book whilst the rest of us braved the winds to explore on foot. At home, I continued to enjoy the same freedom to play outdoors. Our road was in the form of an oval, surrounded by a larger fringe of trees and grass, a fabulous place full of private corners and dens where we could play at any time. My group of friends had a game named 'meet and tell lies', which was just that, though I cannot recall exactly what the objective was, and it had us running around the woodland in circles of detection and deceit. I imagine it was a good preparation for life.

I went on to the local grammar school, where I got a solid, traditional education. There was the occasional inspiring teacher, and I particularly remember the French teacher, but I had decided on medicine fairly early on, which unfortunately meant studying physics and chemistry to A level. My father's help with this homework was vital to my getting through.

Six weeks before my A levels my father died in a road accident. He was in his employer's car and the driver, going too fast, drove headlong into a Smiths Crisps lorry. The three men in the car died instantly. I choose not to describe the aftermath.

The utter loss of my two loved ones has remained ineradicably close, there just under the surface of everything, always ready to come up and colour my thoughts or actions. Unexpected, violent and premature death is the hardest and I have not dealt with it too well.

After that, rather too soon really, I started at university in London. First impressions of the medical course were formal and daunting. On the first day, the Dean addressed us with these words: 'Ladies and gentlemen, you are about to enter the course to become doctors. You will comport yourselves and dress accordingly.' I imagine no Dean would dare try that today. I was an average student and enjoyed it all despite the sheer quantity of work. Things really speeded up when I started the clinical part, got married in my third year, and found life bursting with good things.

In my last year at university my mother, now living in London, became ill with cancer. She dealt with this by denial, which served her well enough as she was able to carry on a fairly normal life without undue distress for over two years. Until, that is, the last week of her life when she faced reality for the first time and retreated in terror beneath the sheets, unable now to communicate. Her denial had not served me so well because we never had a chance to discuss that I would take over the immense responsibility of caring for the twins, who were now fifteen. I have never resolved for myself whether this was an abrogation of duty on her part, for which she bore responsibility, or an inevitable consequence of her personality which had to be accepted. Anyway, at twenty five and pregnant with my first child, I took on this task together with my husband. We did it with pleasure and a naïve enthusiasm. It was an enlightening experience which reaped both problems and ultimately benefits, and only with hindsight can I now see how unprepared I really was.

Time has passed since then. I have lived another thirty-five years and have enjoyed family life, friendships and career, good times and rewards, all contributing to my present happy state in retirement. The early days however were a rollercoaster ride with a recurrent theme of loss. My memories of early events have become overlaid with a kaleidoscope of later pictures, but of course the early memories have shaped the way I deal with the latter. My inner world is sensitive to loss and my paradox is that the more you want something, the more vulnerable you make yourself, yet if you do not want something badly enough it does not work. For self-preservation, I try nowadays to avoid attaching too much importance to things. I can apply this easily enough to most situations but the potential for loss is also the price you pay for relationships.

Since stopping work I have more time for rumination, too much time, to try and enclose this kaleidoscope of memories, impressions and people from nearly sixty years; enough thinking time to make my moods fluctuate within the day or hour. At first, I was preoccupied with being in a state of not working, after decades of work discipline. I fretted over lost skills, patterns of thought, which had taken so long to learn and were now fast disappearing, and the sense that I had little else to offer. I would then start to think about the companionship of work that I missed, and by extension the other people from all those different phases of my life who, for one reason or another, were no longer around. Then I remind myself that my small personal world, seemingly unique to me, is everyone's experience and utterly unimportant in the scale of things, and it all slips into place. None of it needs to matter and my life, right now, is just what I aimed for. And when I get into this loop I begin really to love my family for all they mean to me, above all else.

The Degraded Audio Signal

When I was a teenager at school I used to make funny mistakes. I would understand something slightly differently from the rest of the class and say something that was out of place, and then they would all laugh at me. Also, when I went to see a play I would spend the first ten minutes or so getting used to the very low volume of the voices. Later at university, I failed to hear an entire lecture course on embryology, which I ascribed to the lecturer's poor diction and my usual habit of sitting at the back, or to the subject being just too tedious to hold my attention. I ignored the fact that everyone else had managed perfectly well. My capacity for self-deception must have been well developed and I did nothing to address my obvious hearing loss. However, I got through the medical course and it was not until my first hospital job as a junior doctor that I was forced to confront it. I was working in Ear, Nose and Throat surgery and the surgeon noticed that I was not hearing his words through the face mask, which of course obscured his lip movements. I explained that I was just over an attack of flu and my hearing was still affected. Quite properly, my excuses were swept aside and I was required to have a hearing test. All was then made clear, scientific and incontrovertible.

The audiogram is a graph which plots sound frequency, ranging from low growls to high squeaks along the horizontal axis, against sound intensity or volume on the vertical axis. On the highest points of this graph are the faintest sounds, only just audible to the normal ear. Normal hearing is recorded as a horizontal line that trips quite happily along the top of the graph, hearing at low volume every frequency from distant thunder to faint birdsong, and most importantly the speech frequencies in between. My line on the audiogram took a large dip in the centre, touching on the speech area but recovering at high frequency. This explained my difficulties. The cause was most likely an inner ear nerve condition, no doubt hereditary (though I knew no one in my family so compromised) and there was nothing that could be done about it. And so I stopped denying my hearing loss.

As I could still manage without a hearing aid, I put the whole thing on a back burner for the next five years, until I was twenty eight. At that point, around the birth of my second son, my hearing seemed to take a further dip and I found quite suddenly that I could no longer cope with everyday situations. Speech had become fuzzy and the birds silent. A new audiogram yielded a line which dived straight through the speech area and by-passed the high frequencies. I now needed a hearing aid and was referred to a private provider: suppliers, I was told, to the Royal Family.

I quickly became quite adept with a hearing aid and it felt like coming back into the world. I was fitted with an aid set into a pair of glasses, where the microphone was fixed on one side arm and the speaker on the other, connected by a fine wire which was glued into a groove right across the central section of the glasses. This arrangement stops feedback, the whining noise that is such an irritant for hearing aid users. However, I hit two problems pretty quickly. First, the glasses came only in a standard design in heavy brown plastic, more suited to an unfashionable male. Also, the wire kept falling out, so that I was doomed to repeated and urgent gluing sessions whenever this happened (and it seemed never to happen at a convenient moment). Strangely, I submitted to wearing this monstrosity for the next twelve years.

My hearing continued its downward path, fortunately at a slower rate, but somehow the aids were not quite keeping up with me, and I sank rather expensively into more and more disability. Eventually I was referred by my GP to a specialist NHS audiological department, where for the first time I got proper assessment and effective aids, free of charge. More time has passed since then, and I now have a line on the audiogram which drops straight off the bottom of the page. However, with the advent of digital aids, technology is now on my side and I cope far better.

Hearing loss has been described as receiving a degraded audio signal. I lose the sharp edges of speech, rather like listening to someone talking through a mouthful of marsh-mallows. This distortion is due to losing the high pitched sounds, such as the consonants 's', 'f', and 't' and some vowel sounds. Even the best aid cannot compete with the normal ear for discrimination, and so I still only pick up about 75 per cent of what is said. This proportion plummets when there is background noise. Background noise is the devil, mechanical or human. An open window, unnoticed by everyone else, lets in a torrent of street noise; in a crowded room, I cannot hear the people I am most interested in.

Context is everything. If I miss a word, I generally slot it into place quite easily and unconsciously, as everyone does, by guesswork within the context. But utter a stand-alone word out of context then I shall miss it, and repeating it for me five or six times will not make a jot of difference until it is rephrased. And please, do not talk to me from another room; the odds are so heavily stacked against my making sense of it as to make it pointless. Yet if I am upstairs who would want to come all the way up just to say that they are making tea and do I want a cup? Sainthood awaits those who live, nicely, with the hearing-impaired.

My powerful aids squeak badly. This feedback announces my arrival like the crocodile in *Peter Pan*. My grandson realised this at one year old and used to say 'Grandma' when he heard the squeak coming from the top of the house. Feedback is due to the sound waves ricocheting around the ear canal and is minimised if the ear mould fits snugly, something which is not easy to achieve. Getting my head close to some other object, for example a wall, also provokes feedback as the sound ricochets off this too. The modern habit of greeting almost total strangers with a kiss, on not one but both cheeks, leads to interesting effects. The other person may possibly not know about my problem. As their head gets within close range of mine, the aid emits this horrid noise, and then it happens again on the other side. Some people carry this off superbly with never a shadow of a reaction, whilst others startle just ever so slightly. I like best the ones who laugh openly.

A hearing loss is hard work, as the disability infiltrates most aspects of living. In general, people want to help but do not know how to unless guided, so it is my job to explain and help people to help me. If only more people could keep it up for the duration of a conversation. It can be difficult too to set up a satisfactory hearing environment with different people in rapidly changing situations. In shops for example, noisy places with hurried assistants, you have to get the assistant on your side pretty quickly if the encounter is not to go sour. Some situations, however, do not seem worth the bother, and for me that is the theatre. I know no more desolate experience than sitting in a theatre full of people creased with laughter, whilst I have no idea what it is all about.

The emotional effects of a hearing loss are wide ranging. I have battled with the sense of exclusion that is the bugbear of deafness. Getting by every day with a hearing loss requires some assertiveness, but it has to be carefully balanced and I am still working on that one. Anxiety, previously about my career, has been replaced by anxiety for the future when I shall be deafer, perhaps with fumbling fingers to manage the aids, and worse, a fumbling brain.

After three and a half decades of hearing loss, I have had fluctuating emotions about my disability, for the most part putting it to the back of my mind, but crumpling at times when the pressure was on. My work made huge communication demands on me and took its toll. Though I am happy to have been able to manage a career whilst having this problem, I am certainly more relaxed since I retired. Above all, a great many people have given me understanding and support over the years and I am grateful.

Call Me Grandma

Becoming a grandmother has eclipsed all else, a huge joy and privilege. There are not too many things you can do twice in life, but now I have met and fallen utterly in love with this new little person, much as I did a generation ago with my own children. I have a stake in this child and the continuity of life has taken on a new meaning.

I was there when my grandson was born, not by original intent but because the birth was going far too slowly and my son and daughter-in-law needed more support. When he finally arrived, pale and briefly silent, my thoughts remained with my daughter-in-law who was by then in far reaches of exhaustion. Perhaps it was my own tiredness, but for a long moment I was not focusing or even feeling anxious about him. I had a sense of needing to know him before I could start worrying about him. This state of numbness did not last long, as I was asked to do the symbolic cutting of the cord, my son having declined as he no longer trusted his own steadiness, and so I started my new love affair.

I have had tremendous pleasure in the small things, the miniature details. When he was new I could sit beside him for long periods and just watch, for all the world like a new mother:

his big beautiful slate grey eyes, soon to turn brown like his mother's, his twitchy nose and mobile mouth, and hands detailed down to the microscopic fingerprints. I would watch him sleep too, his jerky baby movements interspersed with periods of total stillness when, again like a mother, I could not stop myself from feeling surreptitiously for his breath. His baby movements entertained me, from the first purposeful movements ('Do you think he knocked that rattle deliberately?'), to the happy moments when he would bounce about and thrash out with arms and legs, or to the more thoughtful ones when he would rub his feet together slowly and stretch his toes out luxuriously.

Seeing my grandson develop from knowing nothing at all, a blank slate at birth, to his present state of knowingness at two years old, has been wonderful. So too his emotional development, as he establishes his place in the world and has incorporated me into his, gradually aware of me, first a presence, then a known one and ultimately as a loving and loved one, a place of safety.

Following his speech development, too, has been sheer excitement as we have begun to communicate and his little character has emerged. I have watched too his bilingual English-Spanish language acquisition, with joy and amazement at its effortless complexity. He has learned Spanish from his mother and he switches, instinctively and instantaneously, between the two languages. He has gone from entry level to using complicated grammatical structures in two languages in two years flat, and can even get most of his Spanish verbs right! Every stage of his development gives such delight that I just do not want him to grow up too quickly.

When I come to visit, which I do every few weeks as the family lives at some distance across the country, we have our own little world of simple games and outings, and now that we know each other pretty well we are building up a store of private jokes and catchwords. I have the time when I am with him to give my full attention, a luxury his parents do not have, and freed from that daily responsibility I can make Lego tracks, play fantasy games or take time to go to the toy shop for a particular size of little man to fit the miniature motorbike. This is not spoiling, because I decide on the scale of any buying, but it is all about involvement. Whenever he can come to grandma and grandpa's house in London we invent special games here, like making a particular layout of play house under the kitchen table using blankets and kitchen utensils. In future no doubt he will invent his own games specific to our house. In addition to all the fun I am also, quite consciously, making memories for him. Inevitably, our time together must be short, and I want to leave him the sort of warm, individual memories that I have from my own grand-parents. My two children sadly did not have grandparents as they had all died young and this time round I am making quite sure that my grandson knows what it is to have the uncondi-tional love and availability that a grandparent can provide.

Watching his smallness and vulnerability, I have found myself worrying on different fronts. I have become over-cautious of dangers, and am no doubt very irritating to others when I fuss. We all worry about dangers and the fragile world we bring our children into, but there is a reason for my level of anxiety. I have found myself remembering, more than ever, the loss of my baby sister who died over fifty years ago. I felt a primitive relief when my grandson passed the age at which she died. I do not remember my own children evoking this strong reaction and feel vaguely guilty about associating the two babies in this way, that I let my grandson carry this burden. However it has happened, for no reason that I can explain, but the delight and sense of continuity I have experienced in my grandson has brought healing.

These serious thoughts however cannot diminish the joy. And as for the future; the next few years? Nowadays, I have enough free time to see plenty of him, particularly before he gets busy with school life. I shall do my best to keep the balance right, to be there often enough but not too much. What is needed is some official grandma measure, and I shall ask my grandson and his family to advise.

TWO EPILOGUES

A Psychological Perspective

Liz MacRae Shaw

The general territory of thinking about our inner feelings has become more familiar in recent years. We have experienced a kind of global warming of the emotions, lapping around the cooler waters of traditional British reserve. Describing emotional states of mind has of course always been the mainspring of literature; two newer springs from this source are the 'misery memoir' and therapy case studies.

The 'misery memoir' has become a popular new genre after the success of *Angela's Ashes*, Frank McCourt's memoir of his Irish childhood. The best of this genre, for example Angela Ashworth's *Once in a House on Fire*, have an emotional resonance and a poetic form of expression which celebrate the resilience of the human spirit in overcoming the most harsh and bleak of childhood experiences. We have some empathic sense of being alongside the author. The more formulaic examples of these books, where suffering is factually recalled, lack resonance and perhaps appeal to the reader's more voyeuristic tendencies; we are looking at the writer through a layer of glass rather than making a real connection.

The second stream of therapy case studies is one where I have spent much time while working as a counsellor. These studies identify a client's psychological and emotional distress, outline his/her personal history from childhood onwards and explain how the interaction with the therapist affected his/her state of mind. These accounts can be very moving in showing how the two participants struggled through uncertainty to enable the client to achieve lasting insight and beneficial change in life.

So where does 'what it feels like to be me' fit in? It is certainly part of the delta of personal reflection but differs from the two streams I have referred to. It is not as self-consciously literary or dramatised as the memoir; it lacks the technical language and the tendency to see psychological issues as pathological problems as can happen with case studies. The personal reflections in this book are a newer, less colonised landscape. How often do we have the privilege of really hearing in depth about another person's interior life? The contributors are not being written about as therapy clients, nor are they writing as survivors of extreme childhoods. They are a more general and varied group. So how well do the theories developed by psychotherapists over the last century resonate with the individual stories here?

The human brain is a story-seeking missile. From early childhood we seek out stories, starting out with our own personal one. It is how we make sense of who we are. In childhood, if we are fortunate, it is our close family, often especially the mother, who is the guardian of our story. As we grow older we share all or parts of it with those close to us.

But is that sense of connection an illusion? Psychotherapists, from Freud onwards, tend towards a more pessimistic view of the human condition. Freud believed that we are unconsciously programmed to repeat patterns in the hope that next time we can put things right. So if we experienced our parents as critical or cold we will seek out intimate partners, colleagues and friends who share the parental qualities. Like the Flying Dutchman, we are condemned to keep repeating the journey but never to arrive.

However, as these stories show, the liver is not the only organ capable of regeneration. The psyche too can recover and grow. Unlike the Flying Dutchman, the contributors to 'What it feels like to be me' have found peaceful havens through sustaining relationships, music and satisfying occupations. These havens give the respite to develop the painful self-examination which gives us more understanding of the patterns that we create for ourselves.

Another way of looking at the impact of our early life on our psychological development is provided by Donald Winnicott, who was both a psychotherapist and a paediatrician. As babies and small children we are totally dependent on the environment, both emotional and practical, that our parents provide. If that environment is not sensitive enough to respond to the child's need for recognition he/she will not be able to develop his/her true self but will be forced into a premature adjustment to his/her environment. To survive this dislocation he/she adopts a false self: a pretence of coping and being what he/she feels is expected. This bending of the self into an ill-fitting shape leads, in later life, to a sense of unreality and worthlessness. However, if these feelings are acknowledged and grappled with, the submerged true self can be brought to the surface and regenerated, as is demonstrated in some of these accounts.

Another pattern shown in these accounts is the stages of life, both in the individual accounts and also in their arrangement according to the age group of the writer. There have been many psychological interpretations of Shakespeare's 'Seven Ages of Man'. One of the most developed is Erikson's. He identified social and psychological tasks to be tackled at each stage of life, from early childhood through to old age. As Michael Jacobs points out, it is too simplistic to regard these stages in a purely linear way because earlier themes keep appearing later in life in a different guise. He suggests that a more useful metaphor is that of the spiral staircase where each stage is repeated at every turn of the staircase; so, for example, adolescent tasks about identity resurface in adult life.

Erikson's task for adolescence is, 'identity versus role confusion'. This is expressed in the teenage drama of criticising parents as a prelude to separating from them and becoming one's own person. This is a long term project, often extending well into the twenties (as the youngest contributor, Nina, wisely acknowledges). The adolescent task contains a paradox because the teenager's desperate need to be part of the peer group means conforming to the group's uniformity before being able to risk showing too much individuality.

Moving on to adult life, Freud maintained that it was supported by the twin pillars of love and work. Erikson further subdivided adult life into three stages. For young adulthood the theme is 'intimacy versus isolation'. The contributors from this first stage demonstrate the healing powers of close relationships, but shadowing the gains of adulthood are the losses. Some of the wide potential highways imagined in adolescence have turned out to be dead ends and the big moral issues are no longer so clearly defined.

By our third decade onwards, as we move into what the novelist Conrad Williams calls 'life's long, central plateau', we have a sharper perspective on the different aspects of our inner being, the historical me of childhood and teenage years as well as the various personas we show to the world. The middle group of correspondents featured in 'Making sense of it all' are in the period of life where Freud's 'love and work' holds sway. Erikson described the task of this stage as, 'generativity versus stagnation.' Generativity has the immediate meaning of parenthood but also has creative and spiritual dimensions.

Becoming a parent gives us a second chance. If we can make some sense out of our own childhood we can create a better emotional environment for our children. Hopefully too we can reach a more compassionate acceptance of our own parents' shortcomings. Winnicott has many interesting observations on parenting, often expressed in paradoxical form. He writes that, 'there is no such thing as a baby', by which he means that a baby cannot exist in isolation, only in the context of his family relationships. He/she develops from an absolute dependence on an environment adapted to his/her needs into a relative dependence where the parent is the intermediary between the child and the outside world. Later, in the adolescent years the parents have to be killed off, symbolically speaking, as the teenager strives towards independence but at the same time they have to be strong enough to survive their offspring's confrontation. The parent needs to know that 'You sowed a baby and you reaped a bomb.'

Raising children is one important way of expressing creative potential. The correspondents show a range of creative explorations. These can be summed up in two broad ways; one is what Winnicott called, 'the capacity to be alone' and the second is through play. Being able to sustain a reflective relationship with oneself is a creative way of managing the harsh facts of life, what Yalom calls 'the givens of existence'. These givens are: the inevitability of death for each of us and for those we love; the freedom to make our lives as we will; our ultimate aloneness; and finally the absence of any obvious meaning or sense to life.

Donne's famous statement, 'No man is an island, entire of itself', would seem to be the direct opposite of Yalom's view. Perhaps Winnicott's ideas can bridge them. To him play, along with art and spirituality are, 'allied ways towards unification and general integration of the personality.' In other words, I play therefore I am. Two aspects of play used by the contributors are humour and metaphor. Play helps us as adults come to terms with the lifelong interplay of illusion and disillusion in the same way as a child's play helped him/her understand the difference between internal reality and the external reality of the outside world. So maybe the twin qualities, the capacity to be alone and the capacity to be playful, mean that our isolation is reduced. To adapt Donne's dictum, we are joined to the mainland by a tidal causeway, the human understanding that connects us. But we also have to manage the high tides of aloneness.

The oldest group of correspondents in the last section, 'Mulling it over', show how the tension between inner and outer realities continues. The interior world expands. As Helen writes, 'My memories are getting into a muddle. There are too many of them to organise any more and trying to construct a continuous story for them has proved impossible.' For Erikson, the task for the last stage of life is, 'integrity versus despair'. There is a lifetime's worth of accumulated losses – deaths of loved ones, decline in health, unborn children, real and symbolic. How to steer between the rocks of denial and the whirlpool of regrets?

We have to face our naked selves without the comforting roles we clothe ourselves in. For the first time since early childhood we are not distracted by responsibilities. We can live more in the moment and enjoy our capacities both to play and to be alone.

I think that the pleasure of reading all these accounts is in recognising how other people are similar to us and yet so different. Although Yalom wrote about the existential despair of human mortality, he also saw the power of connection. He quotes one of his patients who said, 'Even though you're alone in your boat, it's always comforting to see the lights of the other boats bobbing nearby.' To me the correspondents in this book are those lights.

Bibliography

A. Ashworth (1998). *Once in a House on Fire*. Picador

J. Donne, (1572-1631). *Devotions*

E. Erikson (1965). *Childhood and Society*. Penguin Books

S. Freud (1901). *The Psychopathology of Everyday Life*. Penguin Books

M. Jacobs (1998, 2nd ed.). *The Presenting Past*. OUP

F, McCourt (1996). *Angela's Ashes*. Harper

C, Williams (2007). *The Concert Pianist*. Bloomsbury

D, Winnicott (1971). *Playing and Reality*. Routledge

   '   '   (1975). *Collected Papers: Through Paediatrics to Psychoanalysis*. Routledge

J. Yalom (1991). *Love's Executioner*. Penguin Books

A Scientific Perspective

Professor Horace Barlow

What it feels like to be me is what I experience every minute of my waking life, so why would anyone want to know more about it? It seemed pointless, but then I suddenly realised it was connected with the following question that I have long worried about in the lab. Over the last 50 years or so we have made great progress in understanding what the eye does and how it does it; why then is visual experience itself still so puzzling? My current answer is that when we introspect on our experiences we are exercising an extraordinary faculty that is not quite what we think it is; we are not just delving into our minds for our own benefit, we are opening our minds because this enables us to reveal some of its content to others, and the ability to do this is crucial for the existence of human civilisation; but what it tells us does not necessarily overlap much with the scientific under-standing of vision.

This conclusion changes the whole problem. In the rest of this article I shall first try to explain this new view about intro-spection and consciousness (new to me, that is, for it's difficult to be sure that no one else has ever thought the same); then I shall briefly look at what I regard as earlier, false, beliefs based on Cartesian dualism, and finally I shall ask what the new conclu-sions have to say about, 'What it feels like to be me'.

New Conclusions about Introspection

When one introspects one examines one's own past and present subjective experiences. One's motive for doing so is to dig out some facts or insights about one's personal past history, and it is usually assumed that the chief beneficiary of the findings is oneself, the one who is doing the introspecting. It is this last assumption that I think is wrong; in fact, almost the opposite of the truth: its biological value[1] is to enable one to describe to other people some aspects of the neural activity that has taken place in one's own brain, and the beneficiaries are these other people and the community to which they, and presumably you yourself, belong. An everyday example of the use of introspection may illustrate this.

We frequently ask each other questions like 'Why did you buy pears in the market this morning, rather than apples as we had decided?' A moment's introspection usually enables one to find the answer, and a moment's further reflection tells one that this kind of interchange is extremely important. We expect to ask and receive answers to such questions and we expect to be asked them and to be able to answer them. In this way introspection is the basis for civilised communal life among humans, but from a neurophysiological point of view it is also a very demanding and difficult task to bring about. Even if animals communicate with each other much more freely and frequently than we usually suppose, I doubt if they ask and answer these 'Why did you?' questions, as readily as we do. As for computers, the most they usually achieve is an unsolicited remark such as 'Printer is out of paper'. If you want to ask a question about a mistake made by a computer program, it may require a debugging session lasting hours (sometimes days) to dig out the answer.

Compared with the view that the introspecter is the main beneficiary, this new view places a quite different value on introspection, suggesting that it helps the community, and that any benefits to the individual are indirect. On the earlier view, an introspecter might claim that introspection 'helped me to sort out my life', or to 'find myself', but even if this were true, it would be much less important to humanity at large than the suggested contributions to the community. The new view raises the question of how introspection, if it is an altruistic act, can have survival value for the individual, but remembering first how important the community's welfare is for all its individual members, and second that divulging the results of introspection is optional, there will be a Machiavellian aspect to the distribution of the benefits to be derived from introspection.

To understand how complex and difficult to achieve this new task for introspection must be, first suppose we have a robot capable of being instructed to go to the market, to buy apples, and to return with them. Now consider what you would have to add to that robot's nervous system to make it capable of determining, first that there were no satisfactory apples, then that pears were the closest substitute, then deciding to buy them instead, and then when questioned, reporting the whole sequence of events, including the reason for deviating from the original instructions. If introspection is the faculty of being able to report to others useful bits of knowledge about what's going on in one's own brain, then this is certainly not a simple, obvious and straightforward faculty that can just be added to any brain-like mechanism, as we are apt to assume.

Deliberate introspection allows one to convey to another individual, or to make public, evidence or information that would otherwise remain locked up in one's own brain, and the same is true for simple subjective awareness. If you open your eyes on a new visual scene, for a moment or two you may not comprehend all that it contains, but once you are subjectively aware of the scene's content you can communicate it to others. In this respect, simple conscious awareness is like the result of more profound introspection, but it usually refers to the present, rather than the past.

Of course the individual benefits from the introspections of others, because they too can reveal some of the contents of their own brain to you, where the new evidence and information joins what you have gained from your own experience. Through this process, what you have access to through introspection is not just your own past conscious experience, but includes a great deal that has been derived from the experience of others, and the result is that each of us has access to a store of common knowledge, shared by most members of our own particular herd, tribe or group. Of course we all make mistakes, and what I have called a store of common knowledge is really a store of common conclusions or inferences, not all of which are correct. Nevertheless, this store is essential in everyday life and anyone who fails to have access to it suffers greatly, first because everyone will assume you know it, but also for the following reason:

The Importance of Evidence

Since the time of the ancient Greek philosophers, logic and reason have been regarded as the prime faculties of higher cognitive function, but over the past half-century or so the status of another faculty has been gaining ground and has now come to be regarded by many as the most important of all. This is the ability to draw reliable conclusions from uncertain evidence, or the ability to make rapid, intuitive and reasonably efficient statistical inferences (Murray, Gigerenzer). This is the faculty that I think we recognise colloquially as 'having good judgement'.

Now logic and reason are methods you apply in order to extend the web of knowledge after you have been provided with facts, hypotheses and premises. In contrast, for statistical inference the step of collecting the evidence is crucial because the reliability of the conclusion is strictly limited by how much relevant evidence you have been able to assemble. Obviously, the ability to pool evidence and information in the form of common knowledge, which is the result of the ability of each individual to open his/her mind to others through introspection, enormously increases the evidence available, not just for collective decisions but also for each individual's decisions. Humans also increase the evidence available for their decisions in another way.

When something important happens – the death of a king, a flood, the victory of an army, or technical and intellectual advances such as training horses for human use, inventing the wheel, or the theory of gravitational attraction – humans tend to leave permanent evidence that this has occurred. The result is seen in the store of knowledge that fills our libraries and is tried, tested and taught to new generations of students in our schools and universities. This 'external memory', as it has been called (M Donald, 1991), greatly increases the store of knowledge available to individual humans, and therefore also potentially increases the range and reliability of the decisions they can make.

I have only been able to give here a grossly oversimplified account of the way that human brains come to be filled with models of the world that contain much useful knowledge. There are many aspects that I have hardly mentioned: for example, for education to be possible at all, when the teacher asks 'What happened in 1066?', pupils must be able to introspect and reveal what they think is the required answer in their brains. That kind of education is a simple, mass-production, process; the processes that go on between parent and child, or between children and their friends, are enormously more elaborate, because each individual has a large measure of choice about who it exchanges introspections with, and it is these choices that determine the web through which conscious knowledge spreads. These considerations will be important in the final section of this article, when I go back to the problem: 'What it feels like to be me'.

Although this account has been short, I hope it has convinced you of the basic, simple idea that introspection and consciousness, together with recording, testing and organising the results they produce, are the all-important faculties that have enabled humans to reach their dominant position in the world. It's simply that making your own experience available to other people – i.e. introspection – is the first step towards increasing the amount of evidence available to human beings to use in making decisions, and with more evidence we have been able to make better decisions than other animals: no wonder we have enslaved them! There may be some who have reached a similar conclusion independently, but I don't think this view is very widely accepted: Why not?

A Glance at What Went Wrong

For almost four hundred years we have lived under a spell cast by René Descartes, perhaps unintentionally. The story goes that on a cold morning in the winter of 1619-20, while in the Bavarian army, he shut himself in an oven[2] muttering 'Cogito', and emerged at the end of a day's introspection saying 'ergo sum', with the basis of his philosophy half-complete in his mind. This was not just another good day's work, but has messed us up comprehensively ever since, in two ways. First, it gives intro-spection a rather unsavoury reputation as a solitary inward-searching activity that can, just occasionally, result in oracular nuggets of unquestionable truth; I think the simpler view – that it is the operation that opens one's own mind to others in order to share objective evidence and subjective beliefs – is more attractive, and points with greater accuracy to the true biological advantages it brings.

The second disturbing result of the truths that Descartes claimed to reveal is that they force us to regard the mind as something mysterious and separate from the objective, material brain. Some say that this was a sop to religious orthodoxy: he was really interested in the idea that many mind-like functions of the brain could be carried out by material, physical mechanisms (which we now realise is true), and simply added the piece about a separate, non-material mind in order to avoid the unwanted attentions of religious censors. But whether or not he believed it, it does unfortunately seem to be the case that, once you accept the idea that the mind can exist without a brain, then it is very difficult to reverse that acceptance. I personally don't think dualism makes sense today, and we should say firmly 'No, it is absurd to think of a conscious mind as a separate entity from its bodily brain; consciousness is an integral part of certain brains (mainly human ones), and it enables these brains to generate new types of behaviour'. We can then go ahead and ask the all-important question: What are these new types of behaviour? But that's not such an easy question to answer as might be thought.

Types of Conscious Behaviour

It's easy to compile a long list of things that we can do with consciousness, but we are interested in those that, in addition, we cannot do without consciousness, for these are the tasks that the faculty of consciousness adds. Here we come across a difficulty: I think it is impossible to imagine being unconscious, because imagining is a conscious activity and cannot be combined with unconsciousness. It is therefore impossible to search in our imagination for things we may not be able to do while uncon-scious, such as driving a car. Here is something whose veracity we cannot check introspectively, which is interesting, but as an alternative we can search through the tasks we can do consciously, and simply ask whether it is plausible to suppose that a person would be able to perform that task without the aid of consciousness. Let us test the following assertion in this way:

'Two people cannot hold a proper conversation unless both parties are conscious'.

A valid comment about this might run as follows: 'I'm always conscious myself during such conversations, at least if the conversation is a proper one. As for the person I'm conversing with, I certainly expect them to be conscious, and would not regard it as a proper conversation if he or she were not. Furthermore, I'm keenly alert to this possibility and would feel angry and insulted if I got indications that the other person's attention had lapsed to the level of unconsciousness. So I agree with your assertion for normal conversations, but not necessarily for all attempted conversations'.

I think this is a pretty satisfactory example of something that can be done with consciousness and cannot plausibly be done without it. For brevity I shall call such behaviour zombie-impossible or ZI[3]. To explore this approach further one can write a list of activities such as: day-dreaming, driving a car, reading a book, writing a book, learning to fly, playing the piano, practising scales, playing tennis, practising one's tennis service; then one can take each in turn and judge if it is ZI.

Two points impress me when I go through this exercise. The first has long been recognised, namely that the things that we judge to be ZI tend to be things that require a lot of attention, and this really includes the whole of the above list, except perhaps day-dreaming. But there must be another factor involved, for while reading and writing books would seem totally impossible for zombies, this is less true for practising scales, or one's tennis service. I think this second factor, which I have not seen pointed out, is that activities tend to be ZI when they require one brain to interact with behaviour generated by another brain. As argued above, both parties to a conversation must be fully conscious, so this is doubly ZI, but it's instructive to look at other examples.

Take driving a car; this is something of a test case, for under many conditions a driver's reactions are entirely automatic, require no attention and are therefore entirely zombie-possible. But no one would like to be driven by a zombie, and at quite frequent moments driving must be judged definitely ZI. These moments arise when the driver's full attention is needed to decide between several possible courses of action, and although the difficulty of the decision can arise in many ways, one of them is certainly when the probable actions of another driver have to be taken into account.

I am tempted to speculate that any activities one can introspect about contain elements of ZI-ness. Practising scales, for instance, might seem straightforwardly zombie-possible, but on the rare occasions I do it I sometimes hear the voice of my teacher pointing out the uneven, over-emphasised F-sharps, or some other obvious imperfection; a zombie would not have a teacher's voice lodged in its ear, and if it did, this would make it distinctly less zombie-like. Even when day-dreaming, the zombie-est activity listed above, one is recalled to consciousness by imagined thoughts of one's friends: 'Adrian would hate this heat', or 'Mary would be interested in the contrasting greens of those two bushes'. Conscious minds are richly populated with imagined thoughts and voices of other conscious minds: I am not sure we would be conscious at all if the parts of our brains that carry these imagined thoughts and voices were entirely silent.

New Thoughts on 'What it Feels Like to be Me'

I have been promoting two ideas, that consciousness results from physical activity in a material brain, and that its evolutionary survival value is not to benefit the introspecting brain directly, but to transform a community of introspecting brains by enabling them to explain parts of their subjective experiences to each other, thus increasing the amount of evidence widely available for making decisions. Do these ideas make a difference when thinking about a problem such as what it feels like to be me, or is trying to explain them like telling a randy teenager that sex is for procreation, not just pleasure? Preaching about procreation and pleasure tends to be ignored, because nature was smart enough to incorporate expected sexual pleasure solidly into its plans for procreation, but preaching about the community value of intro-spection and consciousness may be different, because this idea points so clearly to alternative courses of action.

If you think of introspection as an entirely selfish activity, you will be delving around for recollections of what happened to you, or what you did on some occasion, in the hope that these recollections will change the image you have of yourself. I don't deny that this can happen, nor that it can sometimes be genuinely beneficial; but being aware of the community aspects of intro-spection and consciousness opens up new possibilities in the form of possible new questions and possible new actions. What communities do I actually belong to? What communities do I think of myself as belonging to? Which of these do I want to belong to? What do I look like to other members of these commu-nities? What communities might I join? What do I want to look like to them? And so on. The communities one belongs to have an extraordinarily powerful influence on you, whether you like it or not, because they have such a strong influence on the intro-spectable content of one's own consciousness. Most people in reasonably free societies have some freedom of choice about the communities they belong to, or at least about the ones they take seriously, so exercising these choices can transform oneself.

If these views have a vaguely religious feel to them, I cannot in truth deny such a possible origin, for I am the product of religious teachers and ancestors as well as agnostics and a few worthy atheists. But the logical justifications I have given above are materialistic, not theistic; if God has had a hand in making me think the way I do, he has done it without my knowledge, and therefore without any acknowledgement being possible.

I'm still not sure why anyone would want to know what it feels like to be me, but when you next indulge in introspection I hope you recall that human civilisation would not be possible without it, and give the activity due respect.

Footnotes

1. *From an evolutionary viewpoint, the biological value of a feature or characteristic is its survival value – the tendency for those individuals that possess it to survive and leave more offspring than other members of the species.*

2. *Sounds odd, but Bertrand Russell says in a footnote, 'Those who know old-fashioned Bavarian houses assure me that this is entirely credible'.*

3. *A zombie is a corpse revived by witchcraft, and the concept was used by Chalmers, Dennett, Flanagan and others in arguments over qualia in the 1990's*

References

Chalmers, David (1996). *The Conscious Mind: In Search of a Fundamental Theory*. Oxford; Oxford University Press.

Dennett, D. C. (1991). *Consciousness explained*. London: Allan Lane.

Donald, M (1991). *Origins of the modern mind*. Cambridge, Mass; Harvard University Press.

Flanagan, O. (1992). *Consciousness reconsidered*. Boston, Mass: MIT Press.

Gigerenzer, G., & Murray, D. J. (1987). *Cognition as intuitive statistics*. Hillsdale: Lawrence Erlbaum.

Russell, Bertrand (1945). *A History of Western Philosophy*. New York; Simon and Schuster

What Does it Feel Like to be You?

We'd love to know.

www.whatitfeelsliketobeme.com

BOOKS

O is a symbol of the world, of oneness and unity. In different cultures it also means the "eye," symbolizing knowledge and insight. We aim to publish books that are accessible, constructive and that challenge accepted opinion, both that of academia and the "moral majority."

Our books are available in all good English language bookstores worldwide. If you don't see the book on the shelves ask the bookstore to order it for you, quoting the ISBN number and title. Alternatively you can order online (all major online retail sites carry our titles) or contact the distributor in the relevant country, listed on the copyright page.

See our website **www.o-books.net** for a full list of over 500 titles, growing by 100 a year.

And tune in to myspiritradio.com for our book review radio show, hosted by June-Elleni Laine, where you can listen to the authors discussing their books.